ADAM SMITH

(1723—1790)

ENGLISH PHILOSOPHERS

ADAM SMITH

(1723—1790)

BY

J. A. FARRER

AUTHOR OF "PRIMITIVE MANNERS AND CUSTOMS," ETC.

CL Reprints

CL Press | Fraser Institute

CL Press

Published by CL PRESS
A Project of the Fraser Institute
1770 Burrard Street, 4th Floor
Vancouver, BC V6J 3G7 Canada
www.clpress.net

Adam Smith (1723-1790)

By J.A. Farrer

Adam Smith (1723-1790)

was originally published in 1881 by G.P. Putnam's Son's.

First printed: February 2024

Cover image: Cover illustration titled "Gutenberg's Press" by Dave Grey, licensed under a Creative Commons Attribution-NoDerivs 2.0 Generic license.

ISBN: 978-1-957698-10-6

Cover design by John Stephens

Foreword to the republication of Farrer's book on Adam Smith, 2024

By Daniel B. Klein

James Anson Farrer (1849–1925) was a Barrister and writer, who at the age of 32 published a too-forgotten book on Adam Smith's *The Theory of Moral Sentiments* (TMS). The title of Farrer's 1881 book—simply *Adam Smith*—is misleading in that the book is not about the whole of Smith's thought, but only TMS. Farrer's book presents background and many of the main ideas in TMS, quoting amply. The final chapter "Review of the Principal Criticisms of Adam Smith's Theory" runs to 30 pages in length. Farrer draws from Dugald Stewart, James Mackintosh and especially Théodore Simon Jouffroy and Thomas Brown, interlacing their criticisms with suggestions on how Smith might have responded. At the end the book (esp. 196–200), Farrer signals a turn to his own voice and judgment, and renders judgments more or less in line with the many earlier critics of TMS. Farrer's treatment of the criticisms are valuable, both as intellectual historiography and, in its own right, as philosophical criticism of Smith. Those who warm to TMS need to engage and respond to the long and rich lines of serious criticism, lines that include Farrer. My own views on the matter are expressed in my book *Contemplating with Adam Smith*, due out from CL Press in 2024.

PREFACE

BY

THE EDITOR.

THE appearance of the first instalment of the Series of
English Philosophers affords the Editor an opportunity of
defining the position and aim of this and the succeeding
volumes. We live in an age of series : Art, Science,
Letters, are each represented by one or more; it is the object
of the present Series to add Philosophy to the list of subjects
which are daily becoming more and more popular. Had it
been our aim to produce a History of Philosophy in the
interests of any one school of thought, co-operation would
have been well-nigh impracticable. Such, however, is not
our object. We seek to lay before the reader what each
English Philosopher thought and wrote about the problems
with which he dealt, not what we may think he ought to
have thought and written. Criticism will be suggested rather
than indulged in, and these volumes will be expositions rather
than reviews. The size and number of the volumes compiled
by each leading Philosopher are chiefly due to the necessity,
which Philosophers have generally considered imperative, of
demolishing all previous systems of Philosophy before they

commence the work of constructing their own. Of this work of destruction little will be found in these volumes; we propose to lay stress on what a Philosopher did rather than on what he undid. In the summary will be found a general survey of the main criticisms that have been passed upon the views of the Philosopher who forms the subject of the work, and in the bibliographic appendix the reader will be directed to sources of more detailed criticism than the size and nature of the volumes in the Series would permit. The lives of Philosophers are not, as a rule, eventful, the biographies will consequently be brief. It is hoped that the Series, when complete, will supply a comprehensive History of English Philosophy. It will include an Introduction to the Study of Philosophy, by Professor H. Sidgwick.

OXFORD, *Nov.*, 1880.

CONTENTS.

	PAGE
BIOGRAPHICAL SKETCH	1

CHAPTER I.
HISTORICAL INTRODUCTION 22

CHAPTER II.
THE PHENOMENA OF SYMPATHY 29

CHAPTER III.
MORAL APPROBATION, AND THE FEELING OF PROPRIETY . . 33

CHAPTER IV.
THE FEELING OF MERIT AND DEMERIT 46

CHAPTER V.
INFLUENCE OF PROSPERITY OR ADVERSITY, CHANCE, AND CUSTOM
    UPON MORAL SENTIMENTS 56

CHAPTER VI.
THEORY OF CONSCIENCE AND DUTY 72

CHAPTER VII.
THEORY OF MORAL PRINCIPLES 88

CHAPTER VIII.

THE RELATION OF RELIGION TO MORALITY . . . . PAGE 98

CHAPTER IX.

THE CHARACTER OF VIRTUE 107

CHAPTER X.

ADAM SMITH'S THEORY OF HAPPINESS 127

CHAPTER XI.

ADAM SMITH'S THEORY OF FINAL CAUSES IN ETHICS . . 135

CHAPTER XII.

ADAM SMITH'S THEORY OF UTILITY 144

CHAPTER XIII.

THE RELATION OF ADAM SMITH'S THEORY TO OTHER SYSTEMS OF MORALITY 152

CHAPTER XIV.

REVIEW OF THE PRINCIPAL CRITICISMS OF ADAM SMITH'S THEORY 172

ADAM SMITH.

BIOGRAPHICAL SKETCH.

The fame of Adam Smith rests so deservedly on his great work, the *Wealth of Nations*, that the fact is apt to be lost sight of, that long before he distinguished himself as a political economist he had gained a reputation, not confined to his own country, by his speculations in moral philosophy. The *Theory of Moral Sentiments* was first published in 1759, when its author was thirty-six; the *Wealth of Nations* in 1776, when he was fifty-three. The success of the latter soon eclipsed that of his first work, but the wide celebrity which soon attended the former is attested by the fact of the sort of competition that ensued for translating it into French. Rochefoucauld, grandson of the famous author of the *Maxims*, got so far in a translation of it as the end of the first Part, when a complete translation by the Abbé Blavet compelled him to renounce the continuance of his work. The Abbé Morellet—so conspicuous a figure in the French literature of that period—speaks of himself in his *Memoirs* as having been impressed by Adam Smith's *Theory* with a great idea of its author's wisdom and depth of thought.[1]

---

[1] *Mémoires*, i. 244. "Sa Théorie des Sentimens Moraux m'avait donné une grande idée de sa sagacité et de sa profondeur." Yet, according to Grimm, it had no success in Paris. *Corresp.*, iv. 291.

The publication of these two books, the only writings published by their author in his lifetime, are strictly speaking the only episodes which form anything like landmarks in Adam Smith's career. The sixty-seven years of his life (1723-90) were in other respects strangely destitute of what are called "events;" and beyond the adventure of his childhood, when he was carried away by gipsies but soon rescued, nothing extraordinary ever occurred to ruffle the even surface of his existence.

If, therefore, the happiness of an individual, like that of a nation, may be taken to vary inversely with the materials afforded by them to the biographer or the historian, Adam Smith may be considered to have attained no mean degree of human felicity. From his ideal of life, political ambition and greatness were altogether excluded; it was his creed that happiness was equal in every lot, and that contentment alone was necessary to ensure it. "What," he asks, "can be added to the happiness of the man who is in health, who is out of debt, and has a clear conscience?"

To this simple standard, circumstances assisted him to mould his life. His health, delicate in his early years, became stronger with age; necessity never compelled him to seek a competence in uncongenial pursuits; nor did a tranquil life of learning ever tempt him into paths at variance with the laws of his moral being or his country. In several passages of his *Moral Sentiments,* it will appear that he took no pains to conceal his preference for the old Epicurean theory of life, that in case of body and peace of mind consists happiness, the goal of all desire.

But the charm of such a formula of life is perhaps more obvious than its rendering into an actual state of existence. Ease of body does not always come for the wishing; and peace of mind often lies still further from command. The advantage of the formula is, that it sets before us a definite aim, and affords us at any time a measure of the happiness we enjoy or of that we see around us. Judged by this standard, however, the conclusion must be—and it is a conclusion from which Adam Smith does not shrink—that the lot of a beggar may be equal in point of happiness to that of a king.

The result of this Epicurean theory of life on Adam Smith was, fortunately for the world, a strong preference for the life of learning and literature over the professional or political life. He abjured from the first all anxiety for the prizes held out by the various professions to candidates for wealth or reputation. Though sent to Balliol at seventeen as a Snell exhibitioner, for the purpose of fitting himself for service in the Church of England, he preferred so much the peace of his own mind to the wishes of his friends and relations, that, when he left Oxford after a residence of seven years, he declined to enter into the ecclesiastical profession at all, and he returned to Scotland with the sole and simple hope of obtaining through literature some post of moderate preferment more suitable to his inclinations.

Fortune seems to have favoured him in making such a course possible, for after leaving Oxford he spent two years at home with his mother at Kirkaldy. He had not to encounter the difficulties which compelled Hume to practise frugality abroad, in order to preserve his independence. His father, who had died a few months before his birth, had been private secretary to the Principal Secretary of State for Scotland, and after that Comptroller of the Customs at Kirkaldy. Adam Smith was, moreover, an only child, and if there was not wealth at home, there was the competence which was all he desired.

By the circumstances of his birth, his education, like that of David Hume, devolved in his early years upon his mother, of whom one would gladly know more than has been vouchsafed by her son's biographer. She is said to have been blamed for spoiling him, but it is possible that what seemed to her Scotch neighbours excessive indulgence meant no very exceptional degree of kindness. At all events, the treatment succeeded, nor had ever a mother a more devoted son. Her death, which did not long precede his own, closed a life of unremitted affection on both sides, and was the first and greatest bereavement that Adam Smith ever had to mourn. The society of his mother and her niece, Miss Douglas, who lived with them, was all that he ever knew of family life; and when the small circle broke up, as it did at last speedily and with short intervals of survival for those who experienced the grief of the first separation, Adam Smith was well-advanced in years. He survived his mother only six years, his cousin about two; and he had passed sixty when the former died.

It is said, that after a disappointment in early life, Adam Smith gave up all thoughts of marriage; but if he thus failed of the happiest condition of life, it is equally true that he was spared the greatest sorrows of human existence, and a number of minor troubles and anxieties. The domestic economy was entirely conducted by his cousin, and to the philosopher is attributed with more than usual justice all that incapacity for the common details of life with which the popular conception always clothes a scholar. It is said that even the fancy of a La Bruyère has scarcely imagined instances of a more striking absence of mind than might be actually quoted of him;[2] and from boyhood upwards he had the habit of laughing and talking to himself which sometimes led casual observers to inferences not to his credit.

Dugald Stewart, whose somewhat meagre memoir on Adam Smith is the chief authority for all that is known of his life,

---

[2] See, for some anecdotes of this kind, the *Quarterly Review*, vol. xxxvi. 200.

describes him as "certainly not fitted for the general commerce of the world or for the business of active life." The subject of his studies rendered him "habitually inattentive to familiar objects and to common occurrences." Even in company, he was apt to be engrossed with his studies, and would seem, by the motion of his lips as well as by his looks and gestures, to be in all the fervour of composition. In conversation "he was scarcely ever known to start a topic himself," and if he did succeed in falling in with the common dialogue of conversation, "he was somewhat apt to convey his own ideas in the form of a lecture." Notwithstanding these defects, we are told of "the splendour of his conversation," and of the inexhaustible novelty and variety which belonged to it, by reason of his ready adaptation of fanciful theories to all the common topics of discourse.

Of his early years—often the most interesting of any, as indicative of future character—singularly little remains known. Some of those who were the companions of his first school years at Kirkaldy, and who remained his friends for life, have attested the passion he even then had for books and "the extraordinary powers of his memory."

At the age of fourteen he was sent to the University of Glasgow, where his favourite studies were mathematics and natural sciences, and where he attended the lectures of Dr. Hutcheson, who has been called "the father of speculative philosophy in Scotland in modern times," and whose theory of the Moral Sense had so much influence on Adam Smith's own later ethical speculations.

Beyond this reference to his studies, nothing is told of Adam Smith's three years at Glasgow. His whole youth is in fact a blank for his biographer. We hear of no prizes, no distinctions, no friendships, no adventures, no eccentricities of any kind. Nor is it much better with regard to his career at Oxford, to which he was sent by the University of Glasgow at the age of seventeen. Only one anecdote remains, of very doubtful truth, and not mentioned by Dugald Stewart, to the effect that he once incurred rebuke from the college authorities of Balliol for having been detected in his rooms reading Hume's *Treatise on Human Nature*. The story is worth mentioning, if only as an indication of the prevalent idea of Adam Smith's bent of mind in his undergraduate days; and those who, in spite of experience, still hold to the theory, that at the bottom of every story some truth must lie, may gather from this one, that even at college the future friend of the historian was attracted by the bold scepticism which distinguished his philosophy.

It was perhaps by reason of this attraction that at the end of seven years at Oxford Adam Smith declined to take orders. Leaving Oxford, which for most men means an entire change of life, meant for him simply a change in the scene of his studies; a transfer of them from one place to another. Languages, literature, and history, could, he found, be studied as well at Kirkaldy as at the chief seat of learning in England. To Oxford, so different in most colleges now from what it was in those days, he seems never to have expressed or felt the gratitude which through life attached him to Glasgow; and his impressions of the English university have been immortalized by him in no flattering terms in what he has said of it in his *Wealth of Nations*.

After nearly two years spent at home, Adam Smith removed to Edinburgh, where, under the patronage of Lord Kames, so well known in connexion with the Scotch literature of the last century, he delivered lectures on rhetoric and *belles lettres*; and the same subject formed the greater part of his lectures as Professor of Logic at Glasgow, to which post he was elected in 1751, at the age of twenty-eight. The next year he was chosen Professor of Moral Philosophy at the same university ; and the period of thirteen years, during which he held this situation, he ever regarded as the most useful and happy of his life.

Of his lectures at Glasgow only so much has been preserved as he published in the *Moral Sentiments* and *Wealth of Nations* respectively. He divided his course into four parts, the first relating to Natural Theology, the second to Ethics, the third to the subject of Justice and the growth of Jurisprudence, the fourth to Politics. Under the latter head he dealt with the political institutions relating to commerce and all the subjects which enter into his maturer work on the *Nature and Causes of the Wealth of Nations ;* whilst under the second head, he expounded the doctrines which he afterwards published in the *Moral Sentiments.* On the subject of Justice, it was his intention to write a system of natural jurisprudence, " or a theory of the general principles which ought to run through and be the foundation of the laws of all nations." It was to have been an improvement on the work of Grotius on the same subject, and the *Theory of Moral Sentiments* concludes with a promise which, unfortunately, was never fulfilled. " I shall," he says, " in another discourse, endeavour to give an account of the general principles of law and government, and of the different revolutions they have undergone in the different ages and periods of society, not only in what concerns justice, but in what concerns police, revenue, and arms, and whatever else is the object of law. I shall not, therefore, at present, enter into any further details concerning the history of jurisprudence.[*]

One of Adam Smith's own pupils, and afterwards for life one of his most intimate friends, Dr. Millar, professor of law

[*] To this hope he still clung even in the sixth edition of his work, published the year of his death, 1790.

at Glasgow, and author of an excellent work on the Origin
of Ranks, has left a graphic description of the great success
which attended these lectures at Glasgow. " There was no
situation in which the abilities of Mr. Smith appeared to
greater advantage than as a professor. . . . . His reputation
as a professor was accordingly raised very high, and a multitude of students from a great distance resorted to the University, merely upon his account. Those branches of science
which he taught became fashionable at this place, and his
opinions were the chief topic of discussion in clubs and literary
societies. Even the small peculiarities in his pronunciation
or manner of speaking, became frequently the objects of
imitation."

It seems to have been during the early years of his professorship at Glasgow that Adam Smith formed that friendship
with David Hume which forms so pleasing a feature in the
life of both of them, and is so memorable in the history of
literary attachments. There was sufficient sameness in the
fundamental characteristics and opinions of each of them,
together with sufficient differences on minor points, to ensure
the permanence of their mutual affection. Both took the
same interest in questions of moral philosophy and political
economy ; both had a certain simplicity and gentleness of
character ; both held the same ideas of the relation of natural
to revealed religion.

A letter written by Hume to his friend in 1759, on the
occasion of the publication of his *Moral Sentiments*, is of interest, not only as characteristic of the friendship between
them, but as indicative of the good reception which the book
immediately met with from all persons competent to judge of
it. The letter is dated April 12, 1759 :—

" I give you thanks for the agreeable present of your *Theory.*
Wedderburne and I made presents of our copies to such of our

acquaintances as we thought good judges, and proper to spread the reputation of the book. I sent one to the Duke of Argyll, to Lord Lyttleton, Horace Walpole, Soame Jennyns, and Burke, an Irish gentleman, who wrote lately a very pretty treatise on the Sublime. Millar desired my permission to send one in your name to Dr. Warburton. I have delayed writing till I could tell you something of the success of the book, and could prognosticate, with some probability, whether it should be finally damned to oblivion, or should be registered in the temple of immortality. Though it has been published only a few weeks, I think there appear already such strong symptoms, that I can almost venture to foretell its fate. . . . . I am afraid of Lord Kames's *Law Tracts.* A man might as well think of making a fine sauce by a mixture of wormwood and aloes as an agreeable composition by joining metaphysics and Scotch law. . . . . I believe I have mentioned to you already Helvetius's book *de l'Esprit.* It is worth your reading, not for its philosophy, which I do not highly value, but for its agreeable composition. I had a letter from him a few days ago wherein he tells me that my name was much oftener in the manuscript, but that the censor of books at Paris obliged him to strike it out. . . . . But what is all this to my book? say you. My dear Mr. Smith, have patience : compose yourself to tranquillity ; show yourself a philosopher in practice as well as profession ; think on the emptiness, and rashness, and futility of the common judgment of men ; how little they are regulated by reason in any subject, much more in philosophical subjects, which so far exceed the comprehension of the vulgar. . . . . A wise man's kingdom is his own breast ; or, if he ever looks farther, it will only be to the judgment of a select few, who are free from prejudices and capable of examining his work. Nothing indeed can be a stronger presumption of falsehood than the approbation of the multitude ; and Phocion, you know, always suspected himself of some blunder when he was attended with the applauses of the populace.

"Supposing, therefore, that you have duly prepared yourself for the worst by all these reflections, I proceed to tell you the melancholy news, that your book has been very unfortunate, for the public seem disposed to applaud it extremely. It was looked for by the foolish people with some impatience; and the mob of literati are beginning already to be very loud in its praises. Three bishops called yesterday at Millar's shop in order to buy copies and to ask questions about its author. The Bishop of Peterborough said he had passed the evening in a company where he heard it extolled above all books in the world. The Duke of Argyll is more decisive than he uses to be in its favour. I suppose he either considers it an exotic or thinks the author will be serviceable to him in the Glasgow elections. Lord Lyttleton says that Robertson, and Smith, and Bower are the glories of English literature. Oswald protests he does not know whether he has reaped more instruction or entertainment from it. But you may easily judge what reliance can be placed on his judgment who has been engaged all his life in public business, and who never sees any faults in his friends. Millar exults and brags that two-thirds of the edition are already sold, and that it is sure of success. You see what a son of earth that is, to value books only by the profit they bring him. In that view, I believe, it may prove a very good book.

"Charles Townsend, who passes for the cleverest fellow in England, is so taken with the performance that he said to Oswald he would put the Duke of Buccleuch under the author's care, and would make it worth his while to accept of that charge. As soon as I heard this I called on him twice, with a view of talking with him about the matter, and of convincing him of the propriety of sending that young nobleman to Glasgow ; for I could not hope that he could offer you any terms which would tempt you to renounce your professorship. But I missed him. . . . .

" In recompense for so many mortifying things, which nothing but truth could have extorted from me, and which I could easily have multiplied to a greater number, I doubt not but you are so good a Christian as to return good for evil ; and to flatter my vanity by telling me that all the godly in Scotland abuse me for my account of John Knox and the Reformation," &c.

The invitation referred to by Hume in this letter to travel with the Duke of Buccleuch came in about four years time ; and the liberal terms in which the proposal was made, together with the strong temptation to travel, led to a final resignation of the Glasgow professorship.

But here again curiosity is doomed to disappointment ; for Adam Smith wrote no journal of his travels abroad, and he had such an aversion to letter-writing that no records of this sort preserve his impressions of foreign life.[4] Scarcely more than the bare outline of his route is known. Some two weeks at Paris were followed by eighteen months at Toulouse. Then a tour in the South of France was followed by two months at Geneva ; and from Christmas, 1765, to the following October the travellers were in Paris, this latter period being the only one of any general interest, on account of the illustrious acquaintances which the introductions of Hume enabled Adam Smith to make in the French capital.

During this period Adam Smith became acquainted with the chief men of letters and philosophers of Paris, such as D'Alembert, Helvetius, Marmontel, Morellet ; and it is to be regretted that Morellet, who mentions the fact of conversations

---

[4] A few of his letters are published in Lord Brougham's *Account of Adam Smith's Life and Works*, i. 279-89.

between himself, Turgot, and Adam Smith, on subjects of political economy and on several points connected with the great work then contemplated by the latter, should have given us no clue to the influence Turgot may have had in suggesting or confirming the idea of free trade. That the intercourse between them became intimate may at least be inferred from the unverified story of their subsequent literary correspondence; and to Quesnai, the economist, it is known that Adam Smith intended, but for the death of the former, to have dedicated his *Wealth of Nations.* With Morellet, too, Adam Smith seems to have been intimate. The abbé records in his *Memoirs* that he kept for twenty years a pocket-book presented to him as a keepsake by Adam Smith. The latter sent him also a copy of the *Wealth of Nations* ten years later, which Morellet, with his usual zeal for translating, set to work upon at once. The Abbé Blavet, however, was again the first in the field, so that Morellet could not find a publisher. It is worth noticing that Morellet mentions the fact that Adam Smith spoke French very badly, which is not the least inconsistent with his biographer's claim for him of an " uncommonly extensive and accurate knowledge" of modern languages.

The duke and the philosopher, having laid in their companionship abroad the foundation of a friendship which lasted till the death of the latter, returned to London in October, 1766. The next ten years of his life Adam Smith spent at home with his mother and cousin, preparing the work on which his fame now chiefly rests. It was a period of quiet uneventful study, and almost solitude. Writing to Hume, he says that his chief amusements are long and solitary walks by the sea, and that he never felt more happy, comfortable, or contented, in his life. Hume made vain endeavours to tempt him to Edinburgh from his retirement. "I want," he said, "to know what you have been doing, and propose to exact a rigorous account of the method in which you have employed yourself during your retreat. I am positive you are wrong in many of your speculations, especially where you have the misfortune to differ from me. All these are reasons for our meeting."

This was in 1769. Seven years later, 1776, the *Wealth of Nations* appeared, and Hume, who was then dying, again wrote his friend a congratulatory letter. "*Euge! Belle!* I am much pleased with your performance, and the perusal of it has taken me from a great state of anxiety. It was a work of so much expectation, by yourself, by your friends, and by the public, that I trembled for its appearance; but am now much relieved. Not but that the reading of it necessarily requires so much attention, that I shall still doubt for some time of its being at first very popular. But it has depth and solidity, and acuteness, and is so much illustrated by curious facts, that it must, at last, take the public attention. It is probably much improved by your last abode in London. If you were here, at my fireside, I should dispute some of your principles. . . . But these, and a hundred other points, are fit only to be discussed in conversation. I hope it will be soon, for I am in a very bad state of health, and cannot afford a long delay."

This letter seems to have led to a meeting between the two friends, the last before the sad final separation. Of the cheerfulness with which Hume met his death, Adam Smith wrote an account in a letter addressed to Strahan, the publisher, and appended to Hume's autobiography, telling how Hume, in reference to his approaching departure, imagined a conversation between himself and Charon, and how he continued to correct his works for a new edition, to read books of amusement, to converse, or sometimes play at whist with his friends. He also extolled Hume's extreme gentleness of

nature, which never weakened the firmness of his mind nor
the steadiness of his resolutions; his constant pleasantry and
good humour; his severe application to study, his extensive
learning, his depth of thought. He thought that his temper
was more evenly balanced than in any other man he ever
knew; and that, however much difference of opinion there
might be among men as to his philosophical ideas, according
as they happened or not to coincide with their own, there
could scarcely be any concerning his character and conduct.
"Upon the whole," he concluded, "I have always considered
him, both in his lifetime and since his death, as approaching
as nearly to the idea of a perfectly wise and virtuous man as
perhaps the nature of human frailty will permit."

Considering that Hume counted among his friends such
churchmen as Robertson the historian, and Blair, author of
the *Sermons*, Adam Smith's confident belief in the uniformity
of judgment about his friend's character need not appear unreasonable; but, unfortunately, a dignitary of the Church,
author of a *Commentary on the Psalms*, and afterwards Bishop
of Norwich, chose to consider the letter to Strahan a mani-
festo against Christianity, and accordingly published anony-
mously a letter to Adam Smith, purporting to be written
"by one of the people called Christians." The writer claimed
to have in his composition a large proportion of the milk of
human kindness; to be no bigot nor enemy to human learning; and never to have known the meaning of envy or
hatred. Strange then that, at the age of forty-six, Dr. Horne
should have been guilty of a letter, which it would be difficult
to match for injustice of inference, or contemptibility of style,
and which he even thought fit to leave to posterity among his
other published works. He begins: "You have been lately
employed in embalming a philosopher; his *body*, I believe I
must say, for concerning the other part of his nature neither

you nor he seem to have entertained an idea, sleeping or waking. Else it surely might have claimed a little of your care and attention; and one would think the belief of the soul's existence and immortality could do no harm, if it did no good, in a *Theory of Moral Sentiments.* But every gentleman understands his own business best."

The letter, pervaded by the same spirit of banter throughout, is too long to quote at length, but the following extracts contain the leading idea: "Are *you* sure, and can you make *us* sure, that there really exist no such things as God, a future state of rewards and punishments? If so, all is well. Let us *then,* in our last hours, read Lucian, and play at whist, and droll upon Charon and his boat; let us die as foolish and insensible, as much like our brother philosophers the calves of the field and the asses of the desert, as we can, for the life of us. . . . . Upon the whole, doctor, your meaning is good; but I think you will not succeed this time. You would persuade us, by the example of David Hume, Esq., that atheism is the only cordial for low spirits, and the proper antidote against the fear of death."

It is difficult to say whether the puerility or the ignorance displayed in this letter is the greater. Either the writer had never read the *Theory of Moral Sentiments* at all, or he was so little versed in philosophy as to see no difference between Deism and Atheism, two distinct logical contradictories. There is, moreover, not a word in Adam Smith's letter to justify any reference to religious questions at all; and subsequent quotations from the *Moral Sentiments* will abundantly demonstrate the total falsity of the churchman's assumptions. Adam Smith treated his letter with the contemptuous silence it so well deserved. The story quoted by Sir Walter Scott, in an article in the *Quarterly,* that Johnson grossly insulted Adam Smith at a literary meeting in Glasgow, by reason of his dislike for him, as the eulogizer of Hume, is easily shown to rest on no foundation. Hume did not die till 1776, and it was three years earlier that Johnson visited Glasgow.

The two years after the publication of his greatest work Adam Smith spent in London, in the midst of that literary society which we know so well through the pages of Boswell. Then, at the request of the Duke of Buccleuch, he was made one of the Commissioners of Custom in Scotland, and in this occupation spent the last twelve years of his life, in the midst of a society which must have formed an agreeable contrast to the long years of his retirement and solitude. The light duties of his office; the pleasures of friendship; the loss of his mother and cousin, and increasing ill-health, all combined to prevent the completion of any more of his literary projects. A few days before his death he ordered all his manuscripts to be burnt, with the exception of a few essays, which may still be read. They consist of a History of Astronomy, a History of Ancient Physics, a History of Ancient Logic and Metaphysics, an Essay on the Imitative Arts, on certain English and Italian verses, and on the External Senses. The destroyed manuscripts are supposed to have comprised the lectures on Rhetoric, read at Edinburgh forty-two years before, and the lectures on Natural Theology and on Jurisprudence, which formed part of his lectures at Glasgow. The additions which he made to the *Moral Sentiments*, in the last winter of his life, he lived to see published before his death.

Of the *Theory of Moral Sentiments* Sir James Mackintosh says: " Perhaps there is no ethical work since Cicero's *Offices*, of which an abridgment enables the reader so inadequately to estimate the merit, as the *Theory of Moral Sentiments*. This is not chiefly owing to the beauty of diction, as in the case of Cicero, but to the variety of explanations of life and manners which embellish the book more than they illuminate the theory. Yet, on the other hand, it must be owned that, for philosophical purposes, few books more need abridgment; for the most careful reader frequently loses sight of principles buried under illustrations. The naturally copious and flowing style of the author is generally redundant, and the repetition of certain formularies of the system is, in the later editions, so frequent as to be wearisome, and sometimes ludicrous."

The justice of this criticism has been the guiding principle in the attempt made in the following chapters to give an account of Adam Smith's system of moral philosophy, the aim having been to avoid sacrificing the main theory to the superabundance of illustration which somewhat obscures it in the original, while at the same time doing justice to the minor subjects treated of, which, though they have little or nothing to do with Adam Smith's leading principles, yet form a distinctive feature in his work, and are in many respects the most interesting part of it; for critics who have rejected the *Theory* as a whole, have been uniformly loud in their praises of its minor details and illustrations. Brown, for instance, who has been the most successful perhaps of all the adverse critics of the *Theory*, speaks of it as presenting in these respects "a model of philosophic beauty." Jouffroy, too, allows that the book is one of the most useful in moral science, because Adam Smith, "deceived as he undoubtedly was as to the principle of morality," brought to light and analyzed so many of the facts of human nature. Dugald Stewart and Mackintosh both say much the same thing; so that it is evident no account of Adam Smith's work can be complete which omits from consideration all the collateral inquiries he pursues or all the illustrations he draws, either from history or from his imagination. To preserve, as far as possible, the proportion which these collateral inquiries bear to one another and to the main theory, as well as to retain

c

what is most characteristic of the original in point of illustration and style, having been therefore the end in view, it has been found best to alter the arrangement in some degree, and to divide the whole into chapters, the relations of which to the divisions of the original will be best understood by a brief reference to the structure of the latter.

Adam Smith divides his work into seven Parts, which precede one another in the following order :—

I. Of the Propriety of Action.

II. Of Merit and Demerit ; or the objects of Reward and Punishment.

III. Of the Foundation of our judgments concerning our own Sentiments and Conduct, and of the Sense of Duty.

IV. Of the Effect of Utility upon the sentiment of Approbation.

V. Of the influence of Custom and Fashion upon the sentiments of Moral Approbation and Disapprobation.

VI. Of the character of Virtue.

VII. Of systems of Moral Philosophy.

The excellence of this arrangement, however, is considerably marred by the division of these Parts into Sections, and by the frequent further subdivison of the Sections themselves into Chapters. An instance will illustrate how detrimental this is to the clearness of the main argument. The first three Parts exhaust the main theory, or that doctrine of Sympathy, which is Adam Smith's own special creation, and on which his rank as a moral philosopher depends; the other four Parts having only to do with it incidentally or by accident. But in following the first three Parts in which the doctrine of Sympathy is expounded, we come across sections which also are only connected incidentally with the leading argument, and are really branches off the main line. Thus in the Part devoted to the explanation of our ideas of Propriety

in Action there occurs a section on the effect of prosperity or
adversity in influencing our judgment; in the Part treating
of Merit and Demerit there is a section on the influence of
fortune or accident on our sentiments of men's merit or the
contrary; and there is, lastly, a distinct Part (Part V.)
allotted to the consideration of the influence of Custom and
Fashion on our sentiments of moral approbation or disapprobation.   These subjects are obviously so nearly allied, that they
might all have been treated together, apart from the doctrine
of sympathy of which they are quite independent; and accordingly in the sequel the dissertations concerning them in
the original are collected into a single chapter, the fifth, on
the influence of Prosperity and Adversity, Chance and Custom,
on our moral sentiments.

Consistently with the principles already explained, the order
of the original has been followed as closely as possible.   The
second, third, and fourth chapters comprise Parts I. and II.
Part V., and the sections relating to the same subject in Parts
I. and II., make up the fifth chapter.   Then Part III. is divided
for clearness' sake into two chapters, explaining the author's
Theory of Conscience and Theory of Moral Principles; and the
end of these two chapters, the sixth and seventh, concludes
the most important half of Adam Smith's treatise.

Part VI., on the Character of Virtue, which forms so large
a division in the original, and which was only added to the
sixth edition, corresponds with chapter IX., under the same
title.   Part IV., on the effect of Utility on our moral sentiments, forms chapter XII., in which all that is said on the subject in different passages is brought together.   Part VII., or
Systems of Moral Philosophy, helps in the thirteenth chapter to
throw into clear light the relation of Adam Smith's theory
to other theories of moral philosophy.   The three chapters on
the relation of religion to morality, on the theory of happi-

ness, and on final causes in ethics, correspond with no similar divisions in the original, but are severally collected from different passages in the book, which, scattered through the work, impress upon it a distinctive character, and constitute the chief part of its colouring. The last chapter of all serves to illustrate the historical importance of Adam Smith's work by showing the large part which it fills in the criticisms of subsequent writers.

An accidental coincidence between Adam Smith's theory and a passage in Polybius has unnecessarily been considered the original source of the Theory of Moral Sentiments. The very same passage is referred to by Hume, as showing that Polybius, like many other ancient moralists, traced our ideas of morality to a selfish origin. Yet there is nothing Adam Smith resented more strongly than any identification of his theory with the selfish system of morality. The coincidence is therefore probably accidental; but the passage is worth quoting, as containing in a few lines the central idea of the doctrine about to be considered. Polybius is speaking of the displeasure felt by people for those who, instead of making suitable returns of gratitude and assistance for their parents, injure them by words or actions; and he proceeds to say that " man, who among all the various kinds of animals is alone endowed with the faculty of reason, cannot, like the rest, pass over such actions, but will make reflection on what he sees; and comparing likewise the future with the present, will not fail to express his indignation at this injurious treatment, to which, as he foresees, he may also at some time be exposed. Thus again, when any one who has been succoured by another in time of danger, instead of showing the like kindness to this benefactor, endeavours at any time to destroy or hurt him; it is certain that all men must be shocked by such ingratitude, through sympathy with the resentment of their neighbour; and from an apprehension also that the case may be their own. Aud from hence arises, in the mind of every man, a certain *notion* of the nature and force of duty, in which consists both the beginning and end of justice. In like manner, the man who, in defence of others is seen to throw himself the foremost into every danger, never fails to obtain the loudest acclamations of applause and veneration from the multitude; while he who shows a different conduct is pursued with censure and reproach. And thus it is that the people begin to discern the nature of things honourable and base, and in what consists the difference between them; and to perceive that the former, on account of the advantage that attends them, are to be admired and imitated, and the latter to be detested and avoided."

CHAPTER I.

HISTORICAL INTRODUCTION.

To explain the origin of our ideas of right and wrong, and to find for them, if possible, a solid basis of authority, apart from their coincidence with the dogmas of theology, was the problem of moral philosophy which chiefly occupied the speculation of the last century, and to which Adam Smith's *Theory of Moral Sentiments* was one of the most important contributions. His theory, like all others, must be understood as an answer to the question : How do we come to regard certain actions or states of mind with approval and to condemn their contraries, and on what grounds can we justify our judgments in such matters and hold them to accord universally with the moral judgments of mankind ?

But in order to understand Adam Smith's answer to this question, and his position in the history of thought, it is necessary to refer briefly to the theories of his predecessors down to the time when he took up the thread of the speculation and offered his solution of the problems they had dealt with.

From the time when such problems first became popular in England, two main currents of thought may be detected running side by side in mutual antagonism to one another ; and whilst according to the teaching of the one school the ultimate standard of morality was the interest of the individual himself or the community he belonged to, the aim of the opposite school was to find some basis for morality which should make it less dependent on changes of circumstance and give to its maxims the authority of propositions that should hold true of all times and places.

The names of Locke, Hobbes, Mandeville, and Hume, are associated with the former school; those of Clarke, Price, Lord Shaftesbury, Bishop Butler, and Hutcheson, with the latter; and the difference between them is generally expressed by classing the former together as the Utilitarian, Selfish, or Sceptical School, and the latter as the school of Intuitionalists.

The doctrine of Hobbes, that morality was identical with the positive commands and prohibitions of the lawgiver, and that the law was thus the real ultimate source and standard of all right and wrong, gave rise to several systems which sought in different ways to find for our moral sentiments a less variable and unstable foundation than was implied by such an hypothesis. It was in opposition to such a theory that Clarke and Price, and other advocates of the so-called Rational or Intellectual system, attributed our perception of moral distinctions to intuitions of our intellect, so that the truths of morality might appear, like those of mathematics, eternal and immutable, independent of peculiarities of time and place, and with an existence apart from any particular man or country, just as the definitions of geometry are independent of any particular straight lines or triangles. To deny, for example, that a man should do for others what he would wish done for himself was, according to Clarke, equivalent to a contention that, though two and three are equal to five, yet five is not equal to two and three.

But the same foundation for an immutable morality that Clarke sought for in the human intellect, others sought for in a peculiar instinct of our nature. Thus Lord Shaftesbury postulated the existence of a moral sense, sufficient of itself to.

make us eschew vice and follow after virtue; and this moral
sense, or primitive instinct for good, was implanted in us by
nature, and carried its own authority with it. It judged of
actions by reference to a certain harmony between our affections, and this harmony had a real existence, independent of
all fashion and caprice, like harmony in music. As symmetry
and proportion were founded in nature, howsoever barbarous
might be men's tastes in the arts, so, in morals, an equally
real harmony always presented a fixed standard for our
guidance.

This idea of a Moral Sense as the source and standard of
our moral sentiments was so far developed by Hutcheson, that
the Moral Sense theory of ethics had been more generally
connected with his name than with that of its real originator.
Hutcheson argued that as we have external senses which perceive sounds and colours, so we have internal senses which perceive moral excellence and the contrary. This moral sense had
its analogues in our sense of beauty and harmony, our sympathetic sense, our sense of honour, of decency, and so forth. It
was a primitive faculty of our nature, a factor incapable of
resolution into simpler elements. It could not, for instance,
be resolved into a perception of utility, for bad actions were
often as useful as good ones and yet failed to meet with approbation, nor could it be explained as a mode of sympathy, for
we might morally approve even of the virtues which our
enemies manifested.

Bishop Butler, like his contemporary, Hutcheson, also
followed Lord Shaftesbury in seeking in our natural instincts
the origin of our moral ideas, Conscience with him taking the
place of the Moral Sense, from its being possessed, as he
thought, of a more authoritative character. Conscience, according to Butler, was a faculty natural to man, in virtue
of which he was a moral agent; a faculty or principle of

the human heart, in kind and nature supreme over all others, and bearing its own authority for being so. Using language about it, which we meet again in the *Theory* of Adam Smith, he spoke of it as "God's viceroy," "the voice of God within us," "the guide assigned to us by the Author of our nature." The obligation to obey it therefore rested in the fact of its being the law of our nature. It could no more be doubted that shame was given us to prevent our doing wrong than that our eyes were given us to see with.

It was at this point that Adam Smith offered his solution of the difficulty. For call it Conscience, Moral Sense, or what you will, such expressions are evidently only re-statements of the problem to be explained. To call the fact of moral approbation by such terms was simply to give it other names; and to say that our conscience or moral sense admitted of no analysis was equivalent to saying that our moral sentiments admitted of no explanation. Adam Smith's theory must therefore be understood as an attempt to explain what the Intuitionalist school really gave up as inexplicable; and it represents the reaction against that *à priori* method which they had employed in dealing with moral problems. In that reaction, and in his appeal to the facts of experience, Adam. Smith followed the lead of both Hartley and Hume. Ten years before him, the former, in his *Observations on Man*, had sought to explain the existence of the moral sense, by tracing it back to its lowest terms in the pleasures and pains of simple sensation, and marking its growth in the gradual association of our ideas. And Hume, a few years later, sought to discover "the universal principle from which all censure or approbation was ultimately derived" by the experimental method of inquiry; by comparing, that is, a number of instances of qualities held estimable on the one hand and qualities held blameable on the other, and observing what was the common element of each. From such an inquiry he inferred that those acts were good which were useful and those bad which were injurious, and that the fact of their being useful or injurious was the cause of their goodness or badness.

Thus it will be seen that the question of chief interest in Adam Smith's time was widely different from that which had divided the schools of antiquity. The aim or chief good of life which chiefly occupied them had receded into the background; and the controversy concerned, as Hume declared, "the general foundation of morals," whether they were derived from Reason or from Sentiment, whether they were arrived at by a chain of argument and process of reasoning or by a certain immediate feeling and internal sense.

But round this central question of the origin of our feelings of moral approbation other questions of considerable interest were necessarily grouped. There was the question of the authority and sanction of our moral sentiments, independently of their origin; and there was the question of the ultimate standard or test of moral actions. And these questions involved yet others, as for example: What was the relation of morality to religion? How far did they necessarily coincide, and how far were they independent of each other? Was human nature really corrupt, and to what degree were the ordinary sanctions of this life a sufficient safeguard for the existence of morality? Did happiness or misery, good or evil, really predominate in the world; and was there such a thing as disinterested benevolence, or might all virtue be resolved into self-love and be really only vice under cloak and concealment?

The latter alternative had been the thesis which Mandeville had partly made and partly found popular. In his view the most virtuous actions might be resolved into selfishness, and self-love was the starting-point of all morality. This became therefore, one of the favourite topics of speculation; but it is only necessary to notice Hume's treatment of it, inasmuch as it supplies the first principle of Adam Smith's theory. Hume assumed the existence of a disinterested principle underlying all our moral sentiments. He argued that " a natural principle of benevolence," impelling us to consider the interests of others, was an essential part of human nature. "The very aspect," he said, "of happiness, joy, prosperity, gives pleasure; that of pain, suffering, sorrow communicates uneasiness." And this fellow-feeling with others he had refused to resolve into any more general principle, or to treat as other than an original principle of human nature.

This phenomenon of Sympathy, or fellow-feeling, which we have by nature with any passion whatever of another person, is made by Adam Smith the cardinal point and distinctive feature of his theory of the origin of moral approbation; and the first sentence of his treatise contains therefore not only his answer—one of flat contradiction—to Mandeville, but the key-note to the whole spirit of his philosophy. " How selfish soever," he begins, " man may be supposed, there are evidently some principles in his nature which interest him in the fortune of others, and render their happiness necessary to him, though he derives nothing from it, except the pleasure of seeing it." So that pity or compassion, which Hobbes had explained as the consciousness of a possible misfortune to ourselves similar to that seen to befall another, is, with Adam Smith, a primary, not a secondary, emotion of our nature, an original and not a derivative passion, and one that is purely disinterested in its manifestation.

In the next chapter and the four succeeding ones we shall observe how on this basis of an original instinct of sympathy Adam Smith constructs his explanation of the origin of our moral ideas. With regard to the explanations already offered by previous writers, he believed that they all contained some portion of the truth from the particular point of view taken by each ; and in the explanation which he himself elaborated, he thought that some part or other of his system embraced and coincided with whatever was true in the different theories of his predecessors.

CHAPTER II.

THE PHENOMENA OF SYMPATHY.

THE phenomena of sympathy or fellow-feeling show, according to Adam Smith, that it is one of the original passions of human nature. We see it in the immediate transfusion of an emotion from one man to another, which is antecedent to any knowledge on our part of the causes of another man's grief or joy. It is a primary factor of our constitution as human beings, as is shown in the instinctive withdrawal of our limbs from the stroke we see aimed at another. It is indeed something almost physical, as we see in the tendency of a mob to twist their bodies simultaneously with the movements of a rope-dancer, or in the tendency of some people on beholding sore eyes to feel a soreness in their own.

Sympathy originates in the imagination, which alone can make us enter into the sensations of others. Our own senses, for instance, can never tell us anything of the sufferings of a man on the rack. It is only by imagining ourselves in his position, by changing places with him in fancy, by thinking what our own sensations would be in the same plight, that we come to feel what he endures, and to shudder at the mere thought of the agonies he feels. But an analogous emotion springs up, whatever may be the nature of the passion, in the person principally affected by it; and whether it be joy or grief, gratitude or resentment, that another feels, we equally enter as it were into his body, and in some degree become the same person with him. The emotion of a spectator always corresponds to what, by bringing the case of another home to himself, he imagines should be that other's sentiments.

But although sympathy is thus an instantaneous emotion, and the expression of grief or joy in the looks or gestures of another affect us with some degree of a similar emotion, from their suggestion of a general idea of his bad or good fortune, there are some passions with whose expression no sympathy arises till their exciting cause is known. Such a passion is anger, for instance. When we witness the signs of anger in a man we more readily sympathize with the fear or resentment of those endangered by it than with the provoked man himself. The general idea of provocation excites no sympathy with his anger, for we cannot make his passion our own till we know the cause of his provocation. Even our sympathy with joy or grief is very imperfect, till we know the cause of it : in fact, sympathy arises not so much from the view of any passion as from that of the situation which excites it. Hence it is that we often feel for another what he cannot feel himself, that passion arising in our own breast from the mere imagination which even the reality fails to arouse in his. We sometimes, for instance, blush for the rudeness of another who is insensible of any fault himself, because we feel how ashamed we should have felt had his conduct and situation been ours. Our sorrow, again, for an idiot is no reflection of any sentiment of his, who laughs and sings, and is unconscious of his misery ; nor is our sympathy with the dead due to any other consideration than the conception of ourselves as deprived of all the blessings of life and yet conscious of our deprivation. To the change produced upon them we join our own consciousness of that change, our own sense of the loss of the sunlight, of human affections, and human memory, and then sympathize with their situation by so vividly imagining it our own.

But whatever may be the cause of sympathy, there is no doubt of the pleasure which the consciousness of a concord of feeling produces, and of the pain which arises from a sense of its absence. Some have accounted for this by the principle of self-love, by saying that the consciousness of our own weakness and our need of the assistance of others makes us to rejoice in their sympathy as an earnest of their assistance, and to grieve in their indifference as a sign of their opposition. But both the pleasure and pain are felt so instantaneously, and upon such frivolous occasions, that it is impossible to explain them as a refinement of self-love. For instance, we are mortified if nobody laughs at our jests, and are pleased if they do; not from any consideration of self-interest, but from an instinctive need and longing after sympathy.

Neither can the fact, that the correspondence of the sentiments of others with our own is a cause of pleasure, and the want of it a cause of pain, be accounted for entirely by the additional zest which the joy of others communicates to our own, or by the disappointment which the absence of it causes. The sympathy of others with our own joy may, indeed, enliven that joy, and so give us pleasure; but their sympathy with our grief could give us no pleasure, if it simply enlivened our grief. Sympathy, however, whilst it enlivens joy, alleviates grief, and so gives pleasure in either case, by the mere fact of the coincidence of mutual feeling.

The sympathy of others being more necessary for us in grief than in joy, we are more desirous to communicate to others our disagreeable passions than our agreeable ones. "The agreeable passions of love and joy can satisfy and support the heart without any auxiliary pleasure. The bitter and painful emotions of grief and resentment more strongly require the

healing consolation of sympathy." Hence we are less anxious
that our friends should adopt our friendships than that they
should enter into our resentments, and it makes us much more
angry if they do not enter into our resentments than if they
do not enter into our gratitude.

But sympathy is pleasurable, and the absence of it dis-
tressing, not only to the person sympathized with, but to the
person sympathizing. We are ourselves pleased if we can
sympathize with another's success or affliction, and it pains
us if we cannot. The conciousness of an inability to sympathize with his distress, if we think his grief excessive, gives
us even more pain than the sympathetic sorrow which the most
complete accordance with him could make us feel.

Such are the physical and instinctive facts of sympathy
upon which Adam Smith founds his theory of the origin of
moral approbation and our moral ideas. Before proceeding
with this development of his theory, it is worth noticing again
its close correspondence with that of Hume, who likewise
traced moral sentiments to a basis of physical sympathy.
"Wherever we go," says Hume, "whatever we reflect on or
converse about, everything still presents us with the view of
human happiness or misery, and excites in our breast a sympathetic movement of pleasure or uneasiness." Censure or
applause are, then, the result of the influence of sympathy upon
our sentiments. If the natural effects of misery, such as tears
and cries and groans, never fail to inspire us with compassion
and uneasiness, "can we be supposed altogether insensible or
indifferent towards its causes, when a malicious or treacherous
character and behaviour are presented to us?"

CHAPTER III.

MORAL APPROBATION, AND THE FEELING OF PROPRIETY.

Having analyzed the facts of sympathy, and shown that the correspondence of the sentiments of others with our own is a direct cause of pleasure to us, and the want of it a cause of pain, Adam Smith proceeds to show that the amount of pleasure or pain felt by one man in the conduct or feelings of another is the measure of his approbation or the contrary. The sentiments of any one are just and proper, or the reverse, according as they coincide or not with the sentiments of some one else who observes them. His approbation varies with the degree in which he can sympathize with them, and perfect concord of sentiment means perfect approbation.

Just as a man who admires the same poem or picture that I do, or laughs at the same joke, allows the justice of my admiration or mirth, so he, who enters into my resentment, and by bringing my injuries home to himself shares my feelings, cannot but thereby approve of them as just and proper. According as his sympathetic indignation fails to correspond to mine, according as his compassion falls short of my grief, according, in short, to the degree of disproportion he may perceive between my sentiments and his, does he feel stronger or weaker disapproval of my feelings.

Moral approbation admits of the same explanation as intellectual approbation. For just as to approve or disapprove of the opinions of others is nothing more than to observe their agreement or disagreement with our own, so to approve or disap-

D

prove of their feelings and passions is simply to mark a similar agreement or disagreement existing between our own and theirs.

Consequently the sentiments of each individual are the standard and measure of the correctness of another's, and it is hardly possible for us to judge of another's feelings by any other canon than the correspondent affection in ourselves. The only measure by which one man can judge of the faculty of another is by his own faculty of the like kind. As we judge of another's eyesight, hearing, or reason, by comparison with our own eyesight, hearing, or reason, so we can only judge of another's love or resentment by our own love or our own resentment. If, upon bringing the case of another home to ourselves, we find that the sentiments which it produces in him coincide and tally with our own, we necessarily approve of his as proportioned and suitable to their objects, while if otherwise, we necessarily disapprove of them as extravagant and out of proportion.

Since, then, one point of view in every moral judgment is the "suitableness" which any affection of the heart bears to the cause or object which excites it, the propriety or impropriety of the action, which results from such affection, depends entirely on the concord or dissonance of the affection with that felt sympathetically by a spectator. Hence that part of moral approbation which consists in the sense of the Propriety of a sentiment to its cause (say, of anger to its provocation), arises simply from the perception of a coincidence between the sentiment of the person primarily affected by it and that of the spectator who, by force of imagination, puts himself in the other's place.

Let us take, for instance, as a concrete case, the exhibition of fortitude under great distress. What is the source of our approbation of it? It is the perfect coincidence of another's firmness with our own insensibility to his misfortunes. By his making no demand on us for that higher degree of sensibility which we find to our regret that we do not possess, he effects a most perfect correspondence between his sentiments and ours, which causes us to recognize the perfect propriety of his conduct. The additional element which raises our feeling of mere approbation into one of admiration, is the wonder and surprise we feel at witnessing a degree of self-command far above that usually met with among mankind.

There are, however, several facts which modify our sense of the propriety or impropriety of another person's sentiments by their concord or disagreement with our own, and which it is important to notice.

First of all, it is only when the objects which excite any sentiment bear some direct relation to the person primarily affected by the sentiment or to ourselves as sympathetically affected by it, that any moral judgment of his sentiment arises on our part. For instance, "the beauty of a plain, the greatness of a mountain, the ornaments of a building, the expression of a picture, the composition of a discourse, the conduct of a third person . . . all the general subjects of science and taste, are what we and our companions regard as having no peculiar relation to either of us." There is no occasion for sympathy, or for an imaginary change of situations, in order to produce, with regard to such things, the most perfect harmony of sentiments and affections. Where there is such harmony, we ascribe to a man good taste or judgment, but recognize no degree of moral propriety.

But it is otherwise with anything which more closely affects us. A misfortune or injury to another is not regarded by him and by us from the same point of view as a poem or picture are, for the former cannot but more closely affect him. Hence a correspondence of feeling is much more difficult and much more important with regard to matters which nearly concern him, than with regard to matters which concern neither him nor us, and are really indifferent to our actual interests. We can easily bear with difference of opinion in matters of speculation or taste; but we cease to be bearable to one another, if he has no fellow-feeling for my misfortunes or my griefs; or if he feels either no indignation at my injuries or none that bears any proportion to my resentment of them.

This correspondence of feeling, then, being at the same time so difficult of attainment and yet so pleasurable when attained, two operations come into play : the effort on our part, as spectators, to enter into the sentiments and passions of the person principally concerned, and the effort on his part also to bring his sentiments into unison with ours. Whilst we strive to assume, in imagination, his situation, he strives to assume ours, and to bring down his emotions to that degree with which we as spectators can sympathize. Conscious as he is that our sympathy must naturally fall short of the violence of his own, and longing as he does for that relief which he can only derive from a complete sympathy of feeling, he seeks to obtain a more entire concord by lowering his passion to that pitch which he is sensible that we can assume. Does he feel resentment or jealousy, he will strive to tone it down to the point at which we can enter into it. And by thus being led to imagine how he himself would be affected, were he only a spectator of his own situation, he is brought to abate the violence of his original passion. So that in a sort of meeting-point of sympathy lies the point of perfect propriety, as has been shown in the case of the propriety of fortitude.

On this twofold tendency of our moral nature two different sets of virtues are based. On our effort to sympathize with the passions and feelings of others are founded the gentler virtues of condescension, toleration, and humanity; whilst the sterner virtues of self-denial and self-command are founded on our effort to attune our passions to that pitch of which others can approve. In a union of these two kinds of virtues—in feeling much for others and little for ourselves, in restraining our selfish and indulging our benevolent affections—consists the highest perfection of which human nature is capable.

But how do we pass from a perception of the propriety of these good qualities to a perception of their virtue, for propriety and virtue mean different things? The answer is, that propriety of sentiment which, when displayed in the usual degree, meets with our approbation merely, calls for our admiration and becomes *virtuous* when it surprises us by an unusual, manifestation of it. Admiration is " approbation, heightened by wonder and surprise." " Virtue is excellence, something uncommonly great and beautiful, which rises far above what is vulgar and ordinary." There is no virtue in the ordinary display of the moral qualities, just as in the ordinary degree of the intellectual qualities there are no abilities. For sensibility to be accounted humanity it must exceed what is possessed by the " rude vulgar of mankind ;" and, in like manner, for self-command to amount to the virtue of fortitude, it must be much more than the weakest of mortals is capable of exerting.

There are, in fact, two different standards by which we often measure the degree of praise or blame due to any action, one consisting in the idea of complete propriety or perfection, in comparison with which all human action must ever appear blameable, and the other consisting in that approach to such perfection of which the majority of men are capable. Just in the same way as a work of art may appear very beautiful when judged by the standard of ordinary perfection, and appear full of faults when judged by the standard of absolute perfection, so a moral action or sentiment may frequently deserve applause that falls short of an ideal virtue.

It having thus been shown that the propriety of any sentiment lies in a meeting-point between two different sympathies,
or in a sort of compromise between two different aspects of the
same passion, it is evident that such propriety must lie in a
certain mediocrity or mean state between two extremes, or in just
that amount of passion into which an impartial spectator can
enter. That grief or resentment, for example, is proper which
errs neither on the side of excess or of defect, which is neither
too much nor too little. The impartial spectator, being unable
either to enter into an excess of resentment or to sympathize
with its deficiency, blames the one extreme by calling it " fury,"
and the other by calling it " want of spirit."

On this point it is noticeable that Adam Smith's theory of
Propriety agrees, as he says himself, "pretty exactly" with
Aristotle's definition of Virtue, as consisting in a mean or
Μεσότης between two extremes of excess or defect. For instance, courage, according to Aristotle, lies in the mean state
between the opposite vices of cowardice and rashness. Frugality is a similar avoidance of both avarice and prodigality, and
magnanimity consists in avoiding the extremes of either arrogance or pusillanimity. And as also coincident in every respect
with his own theory of Propriety, Adam Smith claims Plato's
account of virtue given in the *Republic*, where it is shown to
consist in that state of mind in which every faculty confines
itself to its proper sphere without encroaching on that of any
other, and performs its proper office with exactly that degree
of strength which by nature belongs to it.

But it is obvious that the mean state or point of propriety
must be different in different passions, lying nearer to the
excess in some and nearer to the defect in others. And it will
be found that the decency or indecency of giving expression to
our passions varies exactly in proportion to the general disposition of mankind to sympathize with them.

To illustrate the application of this principle, Adam Smith divides all human passions into five different classes. These are the Passions which take their origin from the body, those which take their origin from a particular turn of the imagination, the unsocial Passions, the social Passions, and the selfish Passions. And whatever doubts may be felt as to the truth of Adam Smith's general theory of the origin of moral approbation, there is no doubt of the interest which attaches to his account of the influence of our sympathies in conditioning the nature of our moral sentiments.

1. To begin with the passions which have their origin *from the body.* The bodily passions, such as hunger and thirst, being purely personal, fail to excite any general sympathy, and in proportion to the impossibility of such sympathy is the impropriety or indecency of any strong expression of them. The real origin of our dislike to such passions when we witness them in others, the real reason why any strong expressions of them are so disagreeable, is not the fact that such passions are those which we share in common with the brutes (for we also share with them natural affection and gratitude), but simply the fact that we cannot enter into them, that they are insufficient to command our sympathies.

With the passions which arise from the imagination it is otherwise than with passions which originate from the body. For instance, a disappointment in love or ambition calls forth more sympathy than the greatest bodily evil, for our imagination lends itself more readily to sympathize with the misfortunes affecting the imaginations of others, than is possible in the case of the sufferings of their bodies. Our imagination moulds itself more easily upon the imagination of another than our bodily frame can be affected by what affects his. Thus we can readily sympathize with a man who has lost his fortune, for he only suffers in his imagination, not in his body ;

and we can fancy, just as he does, the loss of dignity, the neglect of his friends, the contempt from his enemies, the dependence, want, and misery which he himself foresees in store for him. The loss of a leg is a more real calamity than the loss of a mistress; but whilst it would be ridiculous to found a tragedy on the former loss, the latter misfortune has given rise to many a fine play. Mere pain never calls forth any lively sympathy, and for that reason there were no greater breaches of decorum committed in the plays of the Greeks, than in the attempt to excite compassion by the representation of physical agonies, as in the cries of Philoctetes,[1] or the tortures of Hippolytus and Hercules. It is on this little sympathy which we feel with bodily pain that is founded the propriety of constancy and patience in its endurance.

2. Where, however, a passion takes its origin *from a particular turn of the imagination*, the imagination of others, not having acquired that particular turn, cannot sympathize with the passion, and so finds it in some measure ridiculous. This is particularly the case with the passion of love. We may sympathize with our friend's resentment, if he has been injured, or enter into his gratitude, if he has received a benefit; but if he is in love, however reasonable we may think it, " the passion appears to everybody, but the man who feels it, entirely disproportioned to the value of the object; and love, though it is pardoned in a certain age, because we know it is natural, is always laughed at because we cannot enter into it. All serious and strong expressions of it appear ridiculous to a third person; and though a lover may be good company to his mistress, he is so to nobody else. He himself is sensible of this; and, as long as he continues in his sober senses, endeavours to treat his own passion with raillery and ridicule. It is the only style

[1] Lessing, in his *Laocoon*, iv. 3, criticizes Adam Smith's remarks on this subject.

in which we care to hear of it, because it is the only style in which we ourselves are disposed to talk of it."

Our philosopher however admits, that though we cannot properly enter into the attachment of the lover, we readily sympathize with his expectations of happiness. Though his passion cannot interest us, his situation of mingled hope and fear interests us, just as in the description of a sea voyage it is not the hunger of the crew which interests us but the distress which it occasions them. When love is interesting on the stage, it is so simply from the distress it occasions. A scene of two lovers, in perfect security, expressing their mutual fondness for one another, would excite laughter and not sympathy. Such a scene is never endured but from concern for the dangers and difficulties foreseen in the sequel, or from interest in the secondary passions—fear, shame, and despair—which are associated with love as a situation, and with which alone we can really sympathize.

3. In the third place come the *unsocial passions*, such as hatred and resentment, with all their modifications. They also are founded on the imagination, but have to be considerably modified before they touch that point of propriety with which an impartial spectator can sympathize. For these passions give rise to a double sympathy, or rather divide our sympathy between the person who feels them and the person who is the object of them. Though we may sympathize with him who has received a provocation, we also sympathize with his adversary, if he becomes the object of undue resentment. We enter into the situation of both, and the fear we feel with the one moderates the resentment we feel with the other. Hence for resentment to attain the mean of propriety, it must be more reduced from its natural degree than almost any other passion; and the greater restraint a man puts on his anger, the more will mankind, who have a very strong sense

of the injuries done to another, enter into and bear with his resentment.

These unsocial passions are, however, necessary parts of human nature, and as on the one hand we cannot sympathize with excessive indignation, so on the other hand we blame and despise a man "who tamely sits still and submits to insults," from our inability to comprehend his insensibility and want of spirit. These passions are therefore useful to the individual, as serving to protect him from insult and injury ; but there is still something disagreeable in them which makes their appearance in others the natural object of our aversion. It is so even when they are most justly provoked. Hence they are the only passions, the mere expression of which does not command our sympathies till we know the cause. The voice of misery, or the sight of gladness, at once communicates to us corresponding sentiments ; but the tones of hatred or resentment inspire us naturally with fear and aversion. For that reason the music, which imitates such passions, is not the most agreeable, its periods being, unlike those which express joy or grief or love, "irregular, sometimes very short, sometimes very long, and distinguished by no regular pauses."

For all these reasons it is very difficult to adjust resentment to the point of propriety demanded by the sympathy of others. The provocation must be such that we should incur contempt for not resenting it ; and smaller offences are better neglected. We should resent more from a sense that mankind expect it of us than from the impulse of the passion itself. There is no passion concerning whose indulgence we should more carefully consider the sentiments of the cool and impartial spectator. Magnanimity, or a regard to maintain our own rank and dignity, can alone ennoble its expression ; and we should show, from our whole manner, that passion has not extinguished our humanity, and that, if we yield to revenge, we do so with reluctance and from necessity.

4. With regard to the *social passions*, such as generosity, humanity, kindness, compassion, or friendship, the facts are quite different. Not only is the mere expression of these sentiments agreeable, but they are made doubly agreeable by a division of the spectator's sympathies between the person who feels them and the person who is the object of them. We enter with pleasure into the satisfaction of both, into the agreeable emotions of the man who is generous or compassionate, and into the agreeable emotions of the man who receives the benefit of his generosity or compassion.

Hence in these passions the point of propriety lies nearer to the excess than to the defect, just as in the opposite passions it lay nearer to the defect. "There is something agreeable even in the weakness of friendship and humanity," and if we blame the too tender mother, the too indulgent father, or the too generous friend, it is always with sympathy and kindness, and with no feeling of hatred or aversion.

5. Between the social and the unsocial passions the *selfish passions* occupy a middle place. These are joy and grief for our own personal good or bad fortune. Since no opposite sympathy can ever interest the spectator against them, their excessive expression is never so disagreeable as excessive resentment; and for the reason that no double sympathy can ever interest us for them, they are never so agreeable as proper humanity and benevolence.

We are, Adam Smith thinks, naturally disposed to sympathize more with our neighbours' small joys than with their great ones, and more with their great sorrows than with their small ones. A man raised suddenly to a much higher position may be sure that the congratulations of his best friends are not perfectly sincere. If he has any judgment, he is sensible of this, and, instead of appearing elated, endeavours to smother his joy, and keep down his elevation of mind. He affects the same plainness of dress, and the same modesty of behaviour, which became him before, and redoubles his attentions to his former friends. So his conduct may meet with our approval, for " we expect, it seems, that he should have more sympathy with our envy and aversion to his happiness than we have with his happiness."

With the smaller joys of life it is different. The ability of the spectators to sympathize with these places the point of propriety in their indulgence much higher. We readily sympathize with habitual cheerfulness, which spreads itself, as it were, by infection. Hence it is hardly possible to express too much satisfaction in the little occurrences of common life, in the company of yesterday evening, in the entertainment generally, in what was said or done, " and in all those frivolous nothings which fill up the void of human life."

It is otherwise with grief, for while small vexations excite no sympathy, deep affliction calls for the greatest. A man will meet with little sympathy, who is hurt if his cook or butler have failed in the least article of their duty; who is vexed if his brother hummed a tune all the time he was telling a story; who is put out of humour by the badness of the weather when in the country, by the badness of the roads when upon a journey, or by want of company and dulness when in town. Grief is painful to ourselves or to others, and we should endeavour either not to conceive it at all about trifles, or to shake it off if we do. There is a certain " malice in mankind which not only prevents all sympathy with little uneasinesses, but renders them in some measure diverting."

But though we all take delight in raillery, and in the small vexations which occur to our companions, our sympathy with

them in case of deep distress is very strong and very sincere.
" If you labour under any signal calamity; if by some extraordinary misfortune you are fallen into poverty, into diseases,
into disgrace and disappointment . . . you may generally
depend upon the sincerest sympathy of all your friends, and,
as far as interest and honour will permit, upon their kindest
assistance too.   But if your misfortune is not of this dreadful
kind, if you have only been a little baulked in your ambition,
if you have only been jilted by your mistress, or are only
henpecked by your wife, lay your account with the raillery of
all your acquaintance."

CHAPTER IV.

THE FEELING OF MERIT AND DEMERIT.

THE sense of the propriety or impropriety of a moral action or sentiment is, according to Adam Smith, only one side of the fact of moral approbation, a sense of their merit or demerit constituting the other side. An action or sentiment is *proper* or *improper* in relation to its cause, or the motive which excites it, whilst it is *meritorious* or the contrary in relation to its effect, or in accordance with its beneficial or hurtful tendency.

It is important to notice this distinction, for it is a protest, as Adam Smith himself declares, against the theories of Dr. Hutcheson and Hume, who, he complains, had considered too much the tendency of affections, their good or bad results, whilst neglecting the relation in which they stood to their causes. This was to overlook the facts of common life, since a person's conduct and sentiments are generally regarded under both these aspects, a man receiving blame for excess of love, or grief, or resentment, not only by reason of the ruinous effects they tend to produce, but also on account of the little occasion that was given for them. It is the want of proportion between a passion and its cause, as well as the sense of its disastrous effects, which make up the whole character of moral disapprobation. Whilst praise or blame are attached to the first aspect of an action or sentiment, a stronger feeling of sympathy or antipathy attaches itself to either in connexion with their effects, a feeling that they deserve reward or punishment, a feeling in other words of their merit or demerit.

As gratitude is the feeling which most directly prompts us to reward another man, and resentment that which most directly prompts us to punish him, an action will call for reward or punishment according as it is the object of either of these feelings. The measure, therefore, of the merit or demerit of any action will be the feeling of gratitude or resentment it excites.

But here again the principle of sympathy must come into play, to decide on the rightfulness of the gratitude or resentment. An action can only seem meritorious or the contrary, as deserving of reward or punishment, if it is the proper and right object of gratitude or resentment; and only that gratitude or resentment can be proper which commands the sympathy of the impartial spectator. That man's action deserves reward as meritorious who to somebody is the object of a gratitude which every human heart is disposed to beat time to, whilst his action seems to deserve punishment as bad who to somebody is the object of a resentment which every reasonable man can sympathize with and adopt. According as everybody who hears of any action would wish to see it rewarded or punished may it fairly be accounted meritorious or the reverse.

In regarding, then, the beneficial or hurtful tendency of actions, our sense of their merit or demerit, due to sympathy with the gratitude or the resentment they respectively excite, appears to arise in the following way.

Sympathizing as we do with the joy of others in prosperity, we also join them in the satisfaction with which they regard the cause of their good fortune. If the cause has been a man, this is more especially the case. We regard him in the same engaging light in which we imagine he must appear to the object of his bounty, whilst our sympathy with the joy of the latter inspires us also with a reflection of the same gratitude he feels.

In the same manner we sympathize not only with the distress or sorrow of another, but with the aversion he feels towards the cause of it. When we see one man oppressed or injured by another, our sympathy with the sufferer only animates our fellow-feeling with his resentment against his oppressor. So we even enter into the imaginary resentment of the slain, and by an illusive sympathy with that resentment which we know he would feel, were he alive, exact vengeance from the criminal who murdered him.

But although our sympathy with the beneficial results of an act may thus lead us to join in the gratitude it occasions, and so to regard it as meritorious or deserving of reward, this is only, as has been said, one side or aspect of complete moral approbation. To constitute the latter, a sense of the propriety of an action must be joined to a sense of its merit; and an action is only then really good when we can sympathize with the motives of the agent as well as with the gratitude his conduct produces. Wherever we cannot enter into the affections of the agent, wherever we cannot recognize any propriety in the motives which influenced him, we fail to sympathize with the gratitude of the person he has befriended. Where, for instance, the greatest benefits have been conferred from the most trivial motives, as where a man gives an estate to another simply because his name or his surname happen to be the same as his own, little gratitude seems due; and consequently the action, though beneficial in its tendency, since it fails to command our complete sympathy, fails to command our complete approbation.

So on the other hand, however hurtful in their tendency a man's actions or intentions may be, if we sympathize with his

motives, that is, if we look upon him as in the right, we can
feel no sympathy with the resentment of the person in-
juriously affected by him.   If he suffers no more than our own
sympathetic indignation would have prompted us to inflict
upon him, we have no fellow-feeling with his suffering, and
consequently no sense of the demerit of the action he regards
with resentment.   It would be impossible, for instance, to
sympathize with the resentment expressed by a murderer
against his judge.   So that to constitute the sentiment of
complete moral disapprobation, there must be impropriety of
motive on the part of the agent as well as a hurtful result to
some one else; or, in other words, for an action to be pro-
nounced by our sympathetic imagination completely bad, it
must be both improper in its motive and injurious in its result.
It is not enough for it to be simply injurious.

It results therefore from this analysis, that a complete
sense of the merit of an action, or the feeling of perfect
moral approbation, is really "a compounded sentiment," made
up of two distinct sympathetic emotions, namely, of a direct
sympathy with the sentiments of the agent, and an indirect
sympathy with the gratitude of those who receive the benefit
of his actions.   Take our sense of the good desert of a particular character in history—Scipio, Timoleon, or Aristides.
In imagination we become those very persons, and, by a direct
sympathy with them, enter into their designs, and feel the
same generous sentiments that they felt.   But we also by an
indirect sympathy feel the benefit of their great actions, and
enter into the gratitude of those who experienced them.   The
sympathetic emotions of gratitude and love, which we thus
feel when we bring home to our own breast the situation of
those originally concerned, account for our whole sense of the
merit of such actions, and for our desire of their meeting with
a fitting recompence.

In the same way a complete sense of the demerit of an action
is a compounded sentiment made up of two distinct emotions;
of a direct antipathy to the sentiments of the agent, and an
indirect sympathy with the resentment of the sufferer. We
feel a direct antipathy to the detestable sentiments which
actuated a Borgia or a Nero, while we sympathize indirectly
with the resentment of those they afflicted. Our sense of the
atrocity of their conduct, and our delight in hearing of its
punishment—in short, our whole feeling of ill desert, and of
the justice of inflicting evil on the person who is guilty of it,
and of making him grieve in his turn—arises from the sympathetic indignation which boils up in our breast whenever
we thoroughly bring home to ourselves the case of the sufferer.

Nor is it any degradation of our sense of the demerit of
actions to ascribe it to our sympathy with the resentment of
another. Resentment is in every respect the counterpart of
gratitude, and if our sense of merit arises from our sympathy
with the one, our sense of demerit may well arise from our
sympathy with the other. Resentment, too, as a principle of
human nature, is only evil when it appears in excess as
revenge; and as it is excessive a hundred times for once that
it is moderate, we are apt to consider it altogether detestable,
because in its ordinary manifestation it is so. But it is not
disapproved of when properly humbled, and entirely brought
down to the level of the sympathetic indignation of the
spectator. When we as bystanders entertain an animosity
corresponding to that of the sufferer, when his resentment in
no respect exceeds our own, when no word nor gesture escapes
him that denotes an emotion more violent than we can share,
and when he never aims at inflicting a punishment severer
than that we should rejoice to see inflicted or would inflict
ourselves, it is impossible that we should not entirely approve
of his sentiments.

It appears then in Adam Smith's theory, that the element of morality in actions only really arises from reference to their tendency. The sentiment or affection of the heart from which all action results may in relation to its cause or motive be regarded as unsuitable or disproportionate, according as it exceeds or falls short of that mean point with which the general observer can sympathize. It may be thus approved or disapproved as proper or improper, but it is not applauded or condemned as moral or immoral. An anger which is out of proportion to the cause of its provocation, a state of joy or sorrow out of keeping with their origin, a generosity or benevolence that seem excessive, are blamed not as immoral, but as out of harmony with the feelings of a spectator. So with reference to the bodily passions, it is the office of temperance to confine them within those limits " which grace, which propriety, which delicacy, and modesty require," (not within those which morality require). It is only when regard is paid to the effects which flow from different actions, that a stronger feeling appears, a feeling not merely of propriety or impropriety, but of their merit or demerit, or in other words, of their moral worth or the contrary.

It is only actions *of a beneficent tendency,* which proceed from proper motives, that are thus meritorious, for such actions alone seem to deserve a reward, from the gratitude they command from a spectator through sympathy. And it is only actions *of a hurtful tendency,* which proceed from improper motives, that seem really wicked, for they alone seem to deserve a punishment, from the resentment they inspire a spectator with by sympathy.

Adam Smith illustrates his theory that the wrongfulness or demerit of actions depends on our sense of their deserving to be punished by the two virtues of beneficence and justice. The mere want of beneficence, the neglect to do the good

expected of one, may give rise to feelings of dislike and disapprobation, but as it does no real positive evil, it provokes
no feeling of sympathetic resentment. Take a case of the
blackest ingratitude, where a man fails to recompense his
benefactor, when the latter stands in great need of his assistance. Every impartial spectator rejects all fellow-feeling
with the selfishness of his motives, and he is the proper object
of the highest disapprobation. Still since he does no positive
hurt, but only neglects to do the good he might, he is the
object of hatred, not of resentment, two passions which differ
in this respect, that whilst the former is called forth by *impropriety* of sentiment and behaviour, the latter is only
provoked by actions which tend to do real and positive hurt to
some particular persons. Ingratitude therefore cannot be
punished. It is improper, and meets with the disapprobation
of the spectator, but it is not wrong or immoral, in the sense
in which it would be, if it went a step further, and raised a
feeling of resentment by actual hurtfulness of tendency
against somebody.

The *proper* degree of beneficence, moreover, as that which
ordinary experience leads us to expect, and also makes the
measure of our praise or blame, is in itself neither praiseworthy
nor blameable. As it is only the defect of ordinary beneficence which incurs our blame, so it is only the excess of it
which deserves our praise. A father, or son, or brother, who
behaves to the correspondent relation neither better nor worse
than the average of mankind do, seems to deserve neither
praise nor blame. His conduct, though it may attain that
point at which we recognize its propriety and so command
our approbation, commands nothing more. It is only when
we are surprised by unexpected, though proper kindness, or
by unexpected and improper unkindness, that it attains the
point of being praiseworthy or the reverse.

Beneficence, when it thus attains a high degree, when it becomes productive of the greatest good, at once becomes the object of the liveliest gratitude, appears to be deserving of the highest reward, and consequently appears as meritorious and praiseworthy.

The virtue of justice differs from that of beneficence in that the violation of it, by doing real and positive hurt to some particular persons, from motives that are disapproved of, is the natural object of resentment, and calls in consequence for punishment. Resentment was given to us "by nature for defence, and for defence only. It is the safeguard of justice and the security of innocence. It prompts us to beat off the mischief which is attempted to be done to us, and to retaliate that which is already done, that the offender may be made to repent of his injustice, and that others, through fear of the like punishment, may be terrified from being guilty of the like offence." As mankind generally approve of the violence employed to avenge the hurt which is done by injustice, so they much more approve of that which is employed to prevent and beat off the injury, and to restrain the offender from hurting his neighbour. Even the person guilty of intending injustice feels that force may be used against him, both by the person he is about to injure, or by others, either to obstruct the execution of his crime, or to punish him when he has executed it.

This fact accounts for the great distinction between justice and all the other social virtues, that we feel a higher obligation to act according to justice than according to friendship, charity, or generosity; and that, while the practice of the latter virtues seems to be left in some measure to our own choice, we feel ourselves to be "in a peculiar manner tied, bound, and obliged to the observation of justice." For we feel that force may, with the utmost propriety, and with the approbation of mankind, be made use of to compel us to observe the rules of the one, but not to follow the precepts of the others.

It is this feeling, then, of the legitimate use of force and punishment which makes us view with so much stronger a sense of disapprobation actions which are unjust—that is, injurious to others—than actions which are merely breaches of that propriety which we like to see observed in the various relationships that connect men together. A father who fails in the ordinary degree of parental affection to a son, or a son who is wanting in filial respect for his father, or a man who shuts up his heart against compassion, incur, indeed, blame; but not that superior degree of blame which relates to actions of a positively hurtful tendency.

But though this superior form of disapprobation attaches itself to acts of injustice, just as a superior form of approbation attaches itself to actions of great beneficence, there is no more merit in the observance of justice than there is demerit in the neglect of beneficence. "There is, no doubt, a propriety in the practice of justice, and it merits upon that account all the approbation which is due to propriety. But as it does no real positive good, it is entitled to very little gratitude. Mere justice is, upon most occasions, but a negative virtue, and only hinders us from hurting our neighbour. The man who barely abstains from violating either the person or the estate or the reputation of his neighbours, has surely very little positive merit. . . . We may often fulfil all the rules of justice by sitting still and doing nothing." As before explained, the sense of the merit of an action is different from the sense of its propriety, and unless an action has both these characteristics, it does not really satisfy the conditions of *morality*.

In proportion, therefore, to the resentment naturally felt by a sufferer from injustice is the sympathetic indignation of the spectator, and the sense of guilt in the agent. But the resentment itself, being proportioned to the evil done by an act, the demerit of an act may be measured by the evil it causes. Death being the greatest evil one man can do to another, and consequently incurring the highest indignation from those connected with the slain man, takes rank as the worst of all crimes. Injuries to a man's property and possessions being less hurtful to him than an injury to his life or person, theft and robbery rank next to murder in atrocity. And as it is a smaller evil to be disappointed of what we have only in expectation than to be deprived of what we have in possession, breach of contract is a less heinous crime than one which attacks a man's actual property.

CHAPTER V.

INFLUENCE OF PROSPERITY OR ADVERSITY, CHANCE, AND
CUSTOM UPON MORAL SENTIMENTS.

In the estimation of Dugald Stewart, the most valuable contribution of Adam Smith to the improvement of moral science is his attempt to account for the irregularity of our moral sentiments, and for their liability to be modified by other considerations, very different from the propriety or impropriety of the affections of the agent, or from their beneficial or hurtful tendency. Adam Smith was, he thinks, the first philosopher to appreciate thoroughly the importance of the difficulty, which is equally great in every theory of the origin of our moral sentiments; namely, that our actual moral sentiments of approbation, or the contrary, are greatly modified by matters extraneous to the intention of the agent; as, for example, by the influence on the act itself of quite fortuitous or accidental circumstances.

There are, first of all, the effects of prosperity and adversity on the moral judgments of men with regard to the propriety of action, whereby it is easier to obtain approbation in the one condition than it is in the other.

In equal degrees of merit there is scarcely any one who does not more respect the rich and great than the poor and humble; and, on the other hand, an equal amount of vice and folly is regarded with less aversion and contempt in the former than it is in the latter. How is this to be explained?

and what is the origin of this perversion of moral sentiment?

The real explanation of it is to be sought in the fact of our sympathetic emotions, which, as they enter more vividly into the joys than into the sorrows of others, feel more pleasure in the condition of the wealthy than in that of the poor. It is agreeable to sympathize with joy, and painful to enter into grief; so that, where there is no envy in the case, our propensity to sympathize with joy is much stronger than our propensity to sympathize with sorrow; and our fellow-feeling for the agreeable emotion approaches nearer to its original intensity than our fellow-feeling for the painful emotion of another person. It is for this reason that we are more ashamed to weep than to laugh before company, though we may often have as real occasion to do the one as the other: we always feel that the spectators are more likely to go along with us in the agreeable than in the painful emotion. Hence our disposition to admire the rich and powerful, and to despise or neglect the poor and lowly, arises from our association of joy and pleasure with the condition of the former, and of pain and distress with that of the latter.

The condition of the former, in the delusive colours of our imagination, seems to be almost the abstract idea of a perfect and happy state. Hence we feel a peculiar satisfaction with the satisfaction we attribute to them. We favour all their inclinations, and forward all their wishes. We are eager to assist them in completing a system of happiness that approaches so near to perfection.

It is from the command which wealth thus has over the sympathetic and agreeable sentiments of mankind that leads to so eager a pursuit and parade of it, and to so strong an aversion to, and concealment of, poverty. To what purpose is all the toil of the world for wealth, power, and pre-emi-

nence? The only advantage really looked to from it is "to
be observed, to be attended to, to be taken notice of with
sympathy, complacency, and approbation;" and the rich man
glories more in his riches, because they naturally draw upon
him the attention of the world, than for any of the other
advantages connected with them. And for the same reason
the poor man is ashamed of his poverty, for though he may
be as well supplied as the rich man with the necessities of
life, he is mortified at being placed out of the sight of mankind, at being treated with neglect, and at being an object of
the antipathy rather than of the sympathy of his fellows.

Rank and distinction are therefore coveted, as setting us in
a situation most in view of general sympathy and attention.
"And thus, place—that great object which divides the wives of
aldermen—is the end of half the labours of human life, and is the
cause of all the tumult and bustle, all the rapine and injustice,
which avarice and ambition have introduced into the world."

And thus, from our natural disposition to admire the rich
and powerful, a different standard of judgment arises about
the propriety of their conduct than that employed about the
behaviour of other men. A single transgression of the rules
of temperance and propriety by a common man is generally
more resented than their constant and avowed neglect by a
man of fashion. In the superior stations of life, the road to
virtue and that to fortune are not always the same, as they
are generally in the middling and inferior stations. In the
latter stations of life success nearly always depends on the
favour and good opinion of equals and neighbours, and these
can seldom be obtained without a tolerably regular conduct.
In them, therefore, "we may generally expect a considerable
degree of virtue; and fortunately for the good morals of
society, these are the situations of by far the greater part of
mankind."

Not only however has prosperity or adversity great influence on our moral sentiments, leading us to see a propriety in a certain course of behaviour in the one condition which we are apt to condemn as improper in the other, but the praise or blame we attach to any action depends to a great extent on the effect upon it of fortune or accident. Although everybody allows that the merit or demerit of actions is still the same, whatever their unforeseen consequences may be, yet, when we come to particular cases, it is clear that our sentiments of merit or demerit are very much affected by the actual consequences which happen to proceed from any action, and that our sense of either of them is thereby enhanced or diminished.

Every action consists of three parts, some one of which must constitute the basis of whatever praise or blame we attribute to it. These three parts are: the intention or affection of the heart, from which the action proceeds; the external movement of the body which this affection causes; and the good or bad consequences which actually flow from it. It is evident that the movement of the body, being often the same in the most innocent as in the most blameable actions — as in the case of shooting at a bird and shooting at a man— cannot be the source of praise or blame. Neither can the accidental consequences of an action, which depend on fortune, not on the agent. The only consequences for which the latter is responsible are those in some way connected with his intention; so that it is to the intention or affection of the heart, to the propriety or impropriety, to the beneficence or hurtfulness of the design, that all praise or blame, all approbation or disapprobation of any kind, must ultimately belong.

The problem then to be explained is the fact that our sense of a man's merit or demerit is at all influenced by results which lie beyond his control, and that we moderate our praise or blame of his conduct according as his good or bad intention fails or not of its intended benefit or injury. The explanation is as follows.

The passions of gratitude and resentment, on which depend our feeling of the merit or demerit of actions, are ultimately based on the bodily sensation of pleasure and pain. They are excited primarily by whatever produces pleasure or pain, even by inanimate objects. " We are angry for a moment even with the stone that hurts us. A child beats it, a dog barks at it, a choleric man is apt to curse it." We should feel guilty of a sort of inhumanity, if we neglected to avenge our friend by the destruction of the instrument that had accidently caused his death. So it is with gratitude. A sailor who mended his fire with the plank that had saved him from shipwreck would seem guilty of an unnatural act, for we should expect him to preserve it with care and affection. So we conceive something like a real love and affection for a snuff-box, or pen-knife, or a stick, to which we have long been accustomed. "The house which we have long lived in, the tree whose verdure and shade we have long enjoyed, are both looked upon with a sort of respect which seems due to such benefactors. The decay of the one, or the ruin of the other, affects us with a kind of melancholy, though we should sustain no loss by it."

Nevertheless to be the proper object of gratitude and resentment, a thing must not only be the cause of pleasure and pain, but itself capable of feeling them in return. Animals therefore are less improper objects of gratitude and resentment than inanimate things. "The dog that bites, the ox that gores, are both of them punished. If they have been the causes of the death of any person, neither the public, nor the relations of the slain, can be satisfied, unless they are put to death in their turn." And on the other hand, animals that have done a great service, are regarded with much gratitude; and we are shocked with the ingratitude of the officer, in the *Turkish Spy*, who stabbed the horse which had carried him across an arm of the sea, lest it should ever distinguish some other person by a similar feat.

But something more is still necessary to the complete gratification of gratitude and resentment than the mere capability for feeling pleasure or pain in return for pain or pleasure caused. The latter must have been caused by design, and there must be a consciousness of design in the return. The object of resentment is chiefly not so much to make our enemy feel pain in his turn, as to make him conscious that he feels it upon account of his past conduct, and to make him repent of that conduct. And the chief object of gratitude is not only to make our benefactor feel pleasure in his turn, but to make him conscious that he meets with that reward on account of his past conduct, and to make him pleased with that conduct.

Hence three different qualifications are necessary to render anything the complete and proper object of gratitude or resentment. It must first of all be the cause of pleasure or pain ; it must secondly be capable of feeling pleasure or pain ; and it must thirdly produce pleasure or pain from a design, approved of in the one case or disapproved of in the other.

Since then the productiveness of pleasure or pain is the primary exciting cause of gratitude or resentment, though the intentions of any person should be ever so proper and beneficent, or ever so improper and malevolent, yet, if he has failed in producing the good or evil he intended, less gratitude or resentment seems due to him, or in other words, less merit or demerit seems to attach to him, because the pleasure or pain, the exciting causes of gratitude or resentment, are in either case wanting. And so, where in a man's intentions there has been no laudable benevolence or blameable malice, but his actions have nevertheless done great good or great evil, then some gratitude or resentment will attach to him, because their exciting causes have been present in either case. But since the consequences of a man's actions rest altogether with fortune, our sentiments of merit or demerit depend to a great extent upon her influence on events, upon her control of the good or bad, the pleasurable or painful results, which flow from our actions.

Thus the irregularity of our moral sentiments concerning the merit or demerit of actions depends ultimately on the accidental amount of pleasure or pain they produce, since these are the primary exciting causes of our gratitude or resentment. Having explained the cause of the phenomenon, it remains to illustrate the effects.

Even the impartial spectator feels in some measure a difference of merit in a man's conduct according as his good intentions have produced or not the results intended by him, although they may only have been defeated by accident. It is indeed common to say, that we are equally obliged to the man who has endeavoured to serve us, as to the man who really has served us; but this saying, " like all other fine speeches, must be understood with a grain of allowance." When all other circumstances are equal, there will always be, even in the best and noblest mind, some difference of affection in favour of the friend who carries out his good intention, as against the friend who fails to do so.

And as the merit of an unsuccessful attempt to do good is diminished by its miscarriage, so is the demerit of an unsuccessful attempt to do evil. Except in the case of treason, the conception of which is in many countries punished as severely as its commission, the mere design to commit a crime is scarcely ever punished as heavily as its actual perpetration.

In hardly any country is the man, who fires a pistol at his enemy but misses him, punished with death, though there is the same degree of depravity in the criminal design as in the criminal action. "The resentment of mankind, however, runs so high against this crime, their terror for the man who shows himself capable of committing it is so great, that the mere attempt to commit it ought in all countries to be capital. The attempt to commit smaller crimes is almost always punished very lightly, and sometimes is not punished at all. The thief, whose hand has been caught in his neighbour's pocket before he had taken anything out of it, is punished with ignominy only. If he had got time to take away a handkerchief, he would have been put to death."[1] The state of the law only reflects the natural feelings of individuals, who feel less resentment when a man has failed in executing the mischief he intended than when he has actually done them an injury.

For the same reason, a man, who has been saved purely by accident from the commission of a crime he intended, though he is conscious that his real guilt, that of his heart, remains the same, considers himself as less deserving of resentment and punishment; and thus all the sense of his guilt is either diminished or destroyed by the mere fact of fortune having favoured him.

Again, as Fortune influences our moral sentiments by lessening the good or evil, the pleasure or pain, intended by our actions, so does she increase our sense of their merit or demerit, beyond what their mere intention would justify, when they happen to give rise to extraordinary pleasure or pain. Even

---

[1] It is remarkable, as characteristic of the difference of feeling between Adam Smith's time and our own, that he should have mentioned this fact in the criminal law of his time, without the slightest comment of disapproval.

when an intention deserves neither praise nor blame, we are conscious of a shade of merit or demerit, according to its agreeable or disagreeable effects on us. We feel a transitory gratitude to the bearer of good tidings, and a transitory resentment to the innocent author of our sorrow. And though we think it barbarous in Tigranes, king of Armenia, to have struck off the head of a man for being the first to announce the approach of an enemy, yet we think it reasonable that, by the custom of all courts, the officer who first brings the news of a victory should be entitled to considerable preferments.

When the negligence of one man causes damage to another, even though his negligence should be no more than a want of extreme circumspection, the law often insists on compensation. In Rome there was a law which compelled any one who, by reason of his horse taking fright and becoming unmanageable, rode over another man's slave, to compensate the loss. The man himself who thus unintentionally hurts another shows some sense of his own demerit by at least offering an apology. Yet why should he make an apology more than any one else? It is because he is aware that the impartial spectator will feel some sympathy with the natural, but unjust, resentment of the person he has accidentally injured.

But the negligence displayed in any action may be so great as to call not merely for blame and censure, but for actual punishment. For we may so far enter into the resentment felt by one man on account of an unintended injury done to him by another, as to approve of his inflicting a punishment on the offender which would have seemed in excess of the demerit of his offence had no unlucky consequences ensued. For instance, though nothing would appear more shocking to our natural sense of equity than to execute a man merely for having carelessly thrown a stone into the street without hurting anybody, yet, if the stone happened to kill anybody, so great would be the effect of this accident on our moral sentiments that, though the man's folly and inhumanity would not be greater in one case than in the other, we should not consider the severest punishment too hard for him. Gross negligence is, therefore, in law almost the same as malicious design. *Lata culpa prope dolum est.*

But our moral sentiments are considerably affected, not only by the fact of the prosperity or adversity of the person whose conduct we judge, and by the influence of fortune or accident on the result of his intentions, but they are also greatly modified by those two great principles of Custom and Fashion, which have caused so wide a difference of opinion about what is blameable or praiseworthy to prevail in different ages and nations. For the virtues of the savage state are different from those of the civilized state, the virtues of one profession are different from those of another, and those again which we admire in youth are different from those we look for in old age.

This fact is due to the influence of custom, or of fashion, which is a species of custom, as the custom of persons of high rank or character. For both these affect our moral sentiments, albeit in a less degree, yet in exactly the same way that they affect our ideas and feelings about beauty in all objects submitted to our observation.

The influence of custom on our ideas of beauty is very great. For whenever two objects have been seen in frequent conjunction together, the imagination acquires a habit of passing easily from the one to the other; and thus, from the mere habit of expecting to see one when we see the other, though there should be no real beauty in their union, we are conscious of an impropriety when they chance to be separated. If even a suit of clothes is without some insignificant but usual orna-

F

ment, such as a button, we are in some measure displeased by its absence.

The fashion of things changes with a rapidity proportioned to the durableness of their material. The modes of furniture change less rapidly than those of dress, because furniture is generally more durable; but in five or six years it generally undergoes a complete revolution, and every man sees its fashion change in many different ways even in his own lifetime. But the productions of such arts as music, poetry, or architecture, being much more lasting, the fashion or custom, which prevails no less over them than over whatever else is the object of taste, may continue unchanged for a much longer time. A building may endure for ages, a beautiful air may be handed down through generations, a poem may last as long as the world, and thus they may all set the fashion of their particular style or taste much longer than the design of a particular mode of dress or furniture. It is only because of the greater permanence of their fashion, which prevents our having much experience of any change in them, that makes it less easy for us to recognize that the rules we think ought to be observed in each of the fine arts are no more founded on reason and the nature of things than they are in the matter of our furniture and dress.

In architecture, for instance, no reason can be assigned beyond habit and custom for the propriety of attaching to each of the five orders their peculiar ornaments. The eye, having been used to associate a certain ornamentation with a certain order, would be offended at missing their conjunction; but it is inconceivable that, prior to established custom, five hundred other forms should not have suited those proportions equally well.

It is the same in poetry. The ancients thought that a certain species of verse was by nature appropriated to a particular species of writing, according to the sentiment or character intended to be described. One kind of verse was fit for grave and another for gay themes, nor could either be interchanged without the greatest impropriety. Yet that which is the verse of burlesque in English is the heroic verse in French, simply because "custom has made the one nation associate the ideas of gravity, sublimity, and seriousness with that measure which the other has connected with whatever is gay, flippant, and ludicrous."

Custom influences our judgment no less with regard to the beauty of natural objects; and the proportions which we admire in one kind of animal are quite different from those we admire in another. Every class of things has a beauty of its own, distinct from that of every other species.

Adam Smith stops short, however, of adopting the theory, so ably advocated in the last century by the Jesuit Buffier, and followed by Sir Joshua Reynolds, that custom is the sole principle of beauty, and that the beauty of every object consists simply in that form and colour which is *most usual* in every particular class of things. According to Buffier, in each species of creatures, that form was most beautiful which bore the strongest character of the general fabric of its species, and had the strongest resemblance to the greater number of the individuals with which it was classed. Hence the most customary form was the most beautiful, and much practice was needed to judge of the beauty of distinct species of things, or to know wherein the middle or most usual form consisted. Hence, too, different ideas of beauty existed in different countries, where difference of climate produced difference of type. Adam Smith so far agrees with this doctrine as to acknowledge that there is scarcely any external form so beautiful as to please, if quite contrary to custom, nor any so deformed as not to be agreeable, if uniformly supported by it;

but he also argues that, independently of custom, we are
pleased by the appearance of the utility of any form—by its
fitness for the purposes for which it was intended. Certain
colours, moreover, are more agreeable than others, even the
first time they are beheld by us; and though he does not lay
the same stress on smoothness as Burke did, who held that
nothing was beautiful that was not smooth, he also admits
that a smooth surface is naturally more agreeable than a rough
one.

The influence of custom and fashion upon our ideas of beauty
generally being so great as has been explained, what is their
influence upon our ideas of beauty of conduct? To this the
answer is, that their influence is perfectly similar in kind,
though not so great, or rather less potent, over morals than it
is over anything else. Although there is no form of external
objects to which custom will not reconcile us, nor fashion
render agreeable to us, the characters or the conduct of a Nero
or a Claudius are what no custom can ever make agreeable, or
other than the objects of our hatred or derision; for the sentiments of moral approbation and disapprobation are founded on
the strongest passions of human nature, and, though they can
be warpt, they can never be perverted.

Just as custom diminishes our sense of the impropriety of
things which we are accustomed to see together, as in the case
of absurdity of dress, so familiarity from youth upwards with
violence, falsehood, and injustice takes away all sense of the
enormity of such conduct; and, on the other hand, when
custom and fashion coincide with the principles of right and
wrong, they enhance our moral ideas and increase our abhorrence for everything evil. "Those who have been educated
in what is really good company—not in what is commonly
called such—who have been accustomed to see nothing in the
persons whom they esteemed and lived with but justice,

modesty, humanity and good order, are more shocked with whatever seems to be inconsistent with the rules which those virtues prescribe."

Custom affords an explanation of the different ideas of good conduct prevalent in different degrees of civilization. For every age and country look upon that degree of each quality which is most usual in those among themselves who are most esteemed as the golden mean of that particular talent or virtue. Their sentiments concerning the degree of each quality that deserves praise or blame vary according to the degree which is most common in their own country and times; thus, that degree of politeness which might be thought effeminate adulation in Russia might be regarded as barbarous rudeness in France.

In general, the style of manners prevalent in any nation is that which is most suitable to its situation. That which is most suitable being, then, that which is naturally most common, different standards arise with regard to the general propriety of behaviour. A savage, in continual danger, or exposed to frequent want, acquires a hardiness of character, an insensibility to the sufferings of himself or others, which is most suitable to the circumstances of his situation, and which affords a very different standard of self-command than that which is either usual or necessary in civilized life. The general security and happiness which prevail in ages of culture, by affording little exercise to contempt of danger, or to the endurance of pain or hunger, enable the virtues which are founded on humanity to be more cultivated than those which are founded on self-denial; so that to complain when in pain, to grieve in distress, to be overcome by love or anger, are not regarded as weaknesses, as they would be in savage life, nor as affecting the essential parts of a man's character.

In the different professions and ages of life the same influ-

ence of custom may be traced. In each rank and profession
we expect a degree of those manners which experience has
taught us to look for in them. As in each species of natural
objects we are pleased with the conformity to the general type,
so in each species of men we are pleased, " if they have neither
too much nor too little of the character which usually accom-
panies their particular condition and situation." Our approbation of a certain kind of military character is founded entirely
on habit; for we are taught by custom to annex to the military profession "the character of gaiety, levity, and sprightly
freedom, as well as of some degree of dissipation." Whatever
behaviour we have been accustomed to see in any order of
men, comes to be so associated with that order, that whenever
we see the one we expect to see the other, and are pleased or
disappointed according as we see it or not. Nevertheless,
there may exist a propriety of professional behaviour, independent of the custom which leads us to expect it; and we
feel that, apart from all custom, there is a propriety in the
gravity of manners which custom has allotted to the profession
of a clergyman.

In the same way different manners are assigned to the different periods which mark human life. In youth we look
for that sensibility, gaiety, and vivacity which experience
teaches us to expect at that age; and at the extreme of life, a
certain gravity and sedateness is the character which custom
teaches us is both most natural and most respectable.

But nevertheless it is necessary not to exaggerate the effects
of custom and fashion on our moral sentiments; for it is more
concerning the propriety or impropriety of particular usages
than about things of the greatest importance that their influence is most apt to cause perversion of judgment. "We
expect truth and justice from an old man as well as from a
young, from a clergyman as well as from an officer; and it is

in matters of small moment only that we look for the distinguishing marks of their respective characters." No society
could subsist a moment if custom could exercise such perversion over our moral sentiments, with regard to the general
style of conduct and behaviour, as it exercises with regard to
the propriety of particular usages. Uninterrupted custom
prevented the philosophers of Athens recognizing the evil of
infanticide; and to say that a thing is commonly done is daily
offered as an apology for what in itself is the most unjust and
unreasonable conduct.

CHAPTER VI.

THEORY OF CONSCIENCE AND DUTY.

THE theory of Hutcheson, that there exists in mankind an inward moral sense concerned with the direct perception of moral qualities in actions just as the sense of hearing or seeing is concerned with the direct perception of sounds or objects, or the theory of Shaftesbury that what we call conscience is a primary principle of human nature irresoluble into other facts, is very different from the theory of Adam Smith, who refers our moral perceptivity to the workings of the instinct of sympathy.

Having accounted for our moral judgments of the actions of others by bringing them to the test of our power to sympathize with them, he proceeds to explain our moral judgments concerning our own acts by a sort of reflex application of the same principle of sympathy. Our sense of duty, our feeling of conscience, arises simply from the application to our own conduct of the judgments we have learned to pass upon others. So that there really exists no moral faculty which is not originally borrowed from without.

In the same manner as we approve or disapprove of another man's conduct, according as we feel that, when we bring his case home to ourselves, we can sympathize or not with his motives ; so we approve or disapprove of our own conduct according as we feel that, by making our case in imagination another man's, he can sympathize or not with our motives. The only way by which we can form any judgment about our own sentiments and motives is by removing ourselves from our own natural station, and by viewing them at a certain distance from us; a proceeding only possible by endeavouring to view them with the eyes of other people, or as they are likely to view them. All our judgment, therefore, concerning ourselves must bear some secret reference either to what are or to what we think ought to be the judgment of others. We imagine ourselves the impartial spectator of our own conduct, and according as we, from that situation, enter or not into the motives which influenced us, do we approve or condemn ourselves.

We do not therefore start with a moral consciousness by which we learn to judge of others, but from our judgments about others we come to have a moral consciousness of ourselves. Our first moral criticisms are exercised upon the characters and conduct of other people, and by observing that these command either our praise or blame, and that we ourselves affect them in the same way, we become anxious in turn to receive their praise and to avoid their censure. So we imagine what effect our own conduct would have upon us, were we our own impartial spectators, such a method being the only looking-glass by which we can scrutinize, with the eyes of other people, the propriety of our own conduct.

Accordingly our sense of personal morality is exactly analogous to our sense of personal beauty. Our first ideas of beauty and ugliness are derived from the appearance of others, not from our own. But as we are aware that other people exercise upon us the same criticism we exercise upon them, we become desirous to know how far our figure deserves their blame or approbation. So we endeavour by the help of a looking-glass to view ourselves at the distance and with the eyes of other people, and are pleased or displeased with the result, according as we feel they will be affected by our appearance.

But it is evident that we are only anxious about our own beauty or ugliness on account of its effect upon others; and that, had we no connexion with society, we should be altogether indifferent about either. So it is with morality. If a human creature could grow up to manhood in some solitary place, without any communication with his own kind, " he could no more think of his own character, of the propriety or demerit of his own sentiments, of the beauty or deformity of his own mind, than of the beauty or deformity of his own face." Society is the mirror by which he is enabled to see all these qualities in himself. In the countenance and behaviour of those he lives with, which always mark when they enter into or disapprove of his sentiments, he first views the propriety or impropriety of his own passions, and the beauty or depravity of his own mind.

The consciousness of merit, the feeling of self-approbation, admits therefore of easy explanation. Virtue is amiable and meritorious, by reference to the sentiments of other men, by reason of its exciting certain sentiments in them; and the consciousness that it is the object of their favourable regards is the source of that inward tranquillity and self-satisfaction which attends it, just as the sense of incurring opposite sentiments is the source of the torments of vice. If we have done a generous action from proper motives, and survey it in the light in which the indifferent spectator will survey it, we applaud ourselves by sympathy with the approbation of this supposed impartial judge, whilst, by a reflex sympathy with the gratitude paid to ourselves, we are conscious of having behaved meritoriously, of having made ourselves worthy of the most favourable regards of our fellow-men.

Remorse, on the other hand, arises from the opposite sentiments; and shame is due to the reflection of the sentiments our conduct will raise in other men. We again regard ourselves from their point of view, and so by sympathizing with the hatred which they must entertain for our conduct, we become the object of our own blame and hatred. We enter into the resentment naturally excited by our own acts, and anticipate with fear the punishment by which such resentment may express itself. This remorse is, of all the sentiments which can enter the human breast, the most dreadful; "it is made up of shame from the sense of the impropriety of past conduct; of grief for the effects of it; of pity for those who suffer by it; and of the dread and terror of punishment from the consciousness of the justly provoked resentment of all rational creatures."

In this consciousness of the accordance or discordance of our conduct with the feelings of others consists then all the pleasure of a good conscience or of self-approbation, or all the pain of remorse or self-condemnation. The one is based on our love of praise, which the comparison of our own conduct with that of others naturally evolves in us, and the other on our aversion to blame, which arises in the same way.

But if a good or bad conscience consisted simply in knowing ourselves to be the objects of praise or blame, we might approve or condemn ourselves irrespective of the correspondence of external opinion with our real merit or demerit. It is not, therefore, *mere* praise or blame that we desire or dread, but praise-worthiness or blame-worthiness; that is to say, to *be* that thing, which, though it should be praised or blamed by nobody, is the proper object of those mental states. We desire the praise not merely of the spectator, but of the impartial and well-informed spectator.

Adam Smith devotes considerable argument to the origin and explanation of this principle of our moral nature, seeking in this way to raise the account he gives of conscience to a higher level than it could attain as a mere reflex from the sympathies of others about ourselves. As from the love or admiration we entertain for the characters of others, we come to desire to have similar sentiments entertained about ourselves, we should have no more satisfaction from a love or admiration bestowed on us undeservedly than a woman who paints her face would derive any vanity from compliments paid to her complexion. Praises bestowed on us either for actions we have not performed or for motives which have not influenced us, are praises bestowed in reality on another person, not on ourselves, and consequently give us no sort of satisfaction.

But for the same reason that groundless praise can give us no solid joy, the mere absence of praise deducts nothing from the pleasure of praise-worthiness. Though no approbation should ever reach us, we are pleased to have rendered ourselves the proper objects of approbation ; and in the same way we are mortified at justly incurring blame, though no blame should ever actually be attached to us. We view our conduct not always as the spectator actually does view it, but as he would view it if he knew all the circumstances. We feel self-approbation or the reverse, by sympathy with sentiments which do not indeed actually take place, but which only the ignorance of the public prevents from taking place, which we know are the natural effects of our conduct, which our imagination strongly connects with it, and which we conceive therefore as properly belonging to it. The satisfaction we feel with the approbation which we should receive and enjoy, were everything known, resembles very much the satisfaction which men feel who sacrifice their lives to anticipate in imagination the praise that will only be bestowed on them when dead, the praise which they would receive and enjoy, were they themselves to live to be conscious of it.

Hence self-approbation, though originally founded on the imaginary approbation of other men, becomes at last independent of such confirmation, and the sense of the perfect propriety of our own conduct comes to need no external testimony to assure us of it. But the love of self-approbation, which is in fact the same as the love of virtue, is still founded on an implied reference to the verdict of persons external to ourselves, and thus the "still small voice" of conscience resolves itself into the acclamations of mankind.

Adam Smith, in accordance with a leading principle of his system, the importance of which will be noticed in a subsequent chapter, traces in this desire on our part for praiseworthiness as apart from our desire of praise, an intention of Nature for the good of society. For though in forming man for society, she endowed him with an original desire to please and an original aversion to offend his fellows, and, by making him to feel pleasure in their favourable, and pain in their unfavourable regards, taught him to love their approbation, and to dislike their disapproval, she yet saw that this mere love of the one, or dislike of the other, would not alone have rendered him fit for society. Since the mere desire for approbation could only have made him wish to *appear* to be fit for society, could only have prompted him to the affectation of virtue, and to the concealment of vice; she endowed him not only with the desire of being approved of, but with the desire of *being* what ought to be approved of, or of being what he himself approves of in other men. So she made him anxious to be really fit for society, and so she sought to inspire him with the real love of virtue and a real abhorrence of vice.

In the same way that we are thus taught to wish to be the objects of love and admiration are we taught to wish not to be the objects of hatred and contempt. We dread blameworthiness, or being really blameworthy, irrespective of all actual blame that may accrue to us. The most perfect assurance that no eye has seen our action, does not prevent us from viewing it as the impartial spectator would have regarded it, could he have been present. We feel the shame we should be exposed to if our actions became generally known; and our imagination anticipates the contempt and derision from which we are only saved by the ignorance of our fellows. But if we have committed not merely an impropriety, which is an object of simple disapprobation, but a heinous crime, which excites strong resentment, then, though we might be assured that no man would ever know it, and though we might believe that there was no God who would ever punish it, we should still feel enough agony and remorse, as the natural objects of human hatred and punishment, to have the whole of our lives embittered. So great, indeed, are these pangs of conscience, that even men of the worst characters, who in their crimes have avoided even the suspicion of guilt, have been driven, by disclosing what could never have been detected, to reconcile themselves to the natural sentiments of mankind. So completely, even in persons of no sensibility, does the horror of blame-worthiness exceed the dread of actual blame.

The fact, Adam Smith thinks, calls for explanation, that while most men of ordinary capacity despise unmerited praise, even men of the soundest judgment are mortified by unmerited reproach. For, however conscious a man may be of his own innocence, the imputation seems often, even in his own imagination, to throw a shadow of disgrace over his character, and if he is brought to suffer the extreme punishment of human resentment, religion alone can afford him any effectual comfort, by teaching him of an approbation, higher and more important than that of humanity. Why, then, is unjust censure so much less indifferent than unmerited praise?

The answer is, that the pain of the one is so much more pungent than the pleasure of the other. A man of sensibility. is more humiliated by just censure than he is elevated by just applause. And it is much easier to rid oneself by denial, of the slight pleasure of unmerited praise, than of the pain of unjust reproach. Though nobody doubts any one's veracity when he disclaims some merit ascribed to him, it is at once doubted if he denies some crime which rumour lays to his charge.

When we are perfectly satisfied with every part of our own conduct, the judgment of others is of less importance to us than when we are in any doubt of the propriety of our actions; and the opinion of others, their approbation or the contrary, is a most serious matter to us, when we are uneasy as to the justice of our resentment or the propriety of any other passion. And, as a rule, the agreement or disagreement of the judgments of other people with our own varies in importance for us exactly in proportion to the uncertainty we feel of the propriety or accuracy of our own sentiments or judgments. Hence it is that poets and authors are so much more anxious about public opinion than mathematicians or men of science. The discoveries of the latter, admitting by nature of nearly perfect proof, render the opinion of the public a matter of indifference; but in the fine arts, where excellence can only be determined by a certain nicety of taste, and the decision is more uncertain, the favourable judgments of friends and the public are as delightful as their unfavourable judgments are mortifying. The sensibility of poets especially is due to this cause; and we may instance the sensibility of Racine, who used to tell his son that the most paltry criticisms had always given him more pain than the highest eulogy had ever given him pleasure: or that of Gray, who was so much hurt by a foolish parody of two of his finest odes, that he never afterwards attempted anything considerable.

It may happen that the two principles of desiring praise and desiring praiseworthiness are blended together, and it must often remain unknown to a man himself, and always to other people, how far he did a praiseworthy action for its own sake, or for the love of praise; how far he desired to deserve, or only to obtain, the approbation of others. There are very few men who are satisfied with their own consciousness of having attained those qualities, or performed those actions, which they think praiseworthy in others, and who do not wish their consciousness of praiseworthiness to be corroborated by the actual praise of other men. Some men care more for the actual praise, others for the real praiseworthiness. It is therefore needless to agree with those " splenetic philosophers " (Mandeville is intended) who impute to the love of praise, or what they call vanity, every action which may be ascribed to a desire of praiseworthiness.

From this distinction between our desire for praise and our desire for praiseworthiness, Adam Smith arrives at the result, that there are, so to speak, two distinct tribunals of morality. The approbation or disapprobation of mankind is the first source of personal self-approbation or the contrary. But though man has been thus constituted the immediate judge of mankind, he has been made so only in the first instance : " and an appeal lies from his sentence to a much higher tribunal, to the tribunal of their own consciences, to that of the supposed impartial and well-informed spectator, to that of the man within the breast, the great judge and arbiter of their conduct." Two sorts of approbation are thus supposed, that of the ordinary spectator, and that of the well-informed one ; or, as it may be otherwise put, of the man without and the man within the breast. Whilst the jurisdiction of the former is founded altogether in the desire of actual praise, and the aversion to actual blame, that of the latter is founded altogether in the desire of really possessing those qualities, or performing those actions which we love and admire in other people, and in avoiding those qualities and those actions which, in other people, arouse our hatred or contempt.

If Conscience, then, which may be defined as "the testimony of the supposed impartial spectator of the breast," originates in the way described, whence has it that very great influence and authority which belong to it? and how does it happen that it is only by consulting it that we can see what relates to ourselves in its true light, or make any proper comparison between our own interests and those of other people?

The answer is, By our power of assuming in imagination another situation. It is with the eye of the mind as with the eye of the body. Just as a large landscape seems smaller than the window which looks out on it, and we only learn by habit and experience to judge of the relative magnitude of objects by transporting ourselves in imagination to a different station, from whence we can judge of their real proportions, so it is necessary for the mind to change its position before we can ever regard our own selfish interests in their due relation to the interests of others. We have to view our interests and another's, "neither from our own place nor from his, neither with our own eyes nor yet with his, but from the place and with the eyes of a third person, who has no particular connexion with either, and who judges with impartiality between us." By habit and experience we come to do this so easily, that the mental process is scarcely perceptible to us, by which we correct the natural inequality of our sentiments. We learn both the moral lesson, and the lesson in

G

vision, so thoroughly, as no longer to be sensible that it has been a lesson at all.

"It is reason, principle, conscience, the inhabitant of the breast, the man within, the great judge and arbiter of our conduct," who alone can correct the natural misrepresentations of self-love, who shows us the propriety of generosity and the deformity of injustice, the propriety of resigning our own greatest interests for the yet greater interests of others, and the deformity of doing the smallest injury to another in order to obtain the greatest benefit to ourselves. But for this correction of self-love by conscience, the destruction of the empire of China by an earthquake would disturb a man's sleep less than the loss of his own little finger, and to prevent so paltry a misfortune to himself he would be willing to sacrifice the lives of a hundred millions of his brethren, provided he had never seen them. It is not the love of our neighbour, still less the love of mankind, which would ever prompt us to self-sacrifice. It is a stronger love, a more powerful affection, " the love of what is honourable and noble, of the grandeur, and dignity, and superiority of our own characters."

The sense of duty in its various forms is the result of the commands of conscience, which thus exists within us as the reflection of external approbation. When the happiness or misery of others depends on our conduct, conscience, or "the man within," immediately calls to us that if we prefer ourselves to them, or the interest of one to the interest of many, we render ourselves the proper object of the contempt and resentment of our fellows.

The control of our passive feelings, of our natural preference for our own interests and our natural indifference to those of others, can only be acquired by a regard to the sentiments of the real or supposed spectator of our conduct. This is the discipline ordained by nature for the acquisition of the virtue of self-command as well as of all other virtues. The whole of life is an education in the acquisition of self-command. A child, as soon as it mixes with its equals at school, wishes naturally to gain their favour and avoid their contempt; and it is taught by a regard to its own safety to moderate its anger and other passions to the degree with which its play-fellows are likely to be pleased. From that time forth, the exercise of discipline over its feelings becomes the practice of its life.

Only the man who has been thoroughly bred in the great school of self-command, the bustle and business of the world, maintains perfect control over his passive feelings upon all occasions. He has never dared to forget for one moment the judgment likely to be passed by the impartial spectator upon his sentiments and conduct, nor suffered the man within the breast to be absent for one moment from his attention. With the eyes of this great inmate he has been accustomed to regard all that relates to himself. From his having been under the constant necessity of moulding, or trying to mould, his conduct and feelings in accordance with those of this spectator, the habit has become perfectly familiar to him; and he almost identifies himself with, he almost becomes himself that impartial spectator; he hardly ever feels but as that great arbiter of his conduct directs.

But with most men conscience, which is founded on the approbation of an imaginary spectator, requires often to be aroused by contact with a real one. " The man within the breast, the abstract and ideal spectator of our sentiments and conduct, requires often to be awakened and put in mind of his duty by the presence of the real spectator." In other words, conscience requires to be kept fresh by contact with the world; solitude leads us to overrate the good actions we may have done or the injuries we may have suffered, and causes us to be too much dejected in adversity as well as too much elated in prosperity.

Nevertheless if the actual spectator is not impartial like the distant one of imagination or reality, the rectitude of our judgments concerning our own conduct is liable to be much perverted; and this fact accounts for many anomalies of our moral sentiments.

Take, for instance, the conduct of two different nations to one another. Neutral nations, the only indifferent and impartial spectators of their conduct, are so far off as to be almost out of sight. The citizen of either nation pays little regard to the sentiments of foreign countries, but only seeks to obtain the approbation of his own fellow-citizens, which he can never do better than by enraging and offending the enemies they have in common. Thus the partial spectator is at hand, the impartial one at a distance. Hence the total disregard in the life of nations of the rules of morality in force in private life. " In war and negotiation the laws of justice are very seldom observed. Truth and fair dealing are almost totally disregarded. Treaties are violated; and the violation, if some advantage is gained by it, sheds scarce any dishonour upon the violator. The ambassador who dupes the minister of a foreign nation is admired and applauded." · The same conduct which in private transactions would make a man beloved and esteemed, in public transactions would load him with contempt and detestation. Not only are the laws of nations violated without dishonour, but they are themselves laid down with very little regard to the plainest rules of justice. It is in the most perfect conformity with what are called the laws of nations that the goods of peaceable citizens should be liable to seizure on land and sea, that their lands should be laid waste, their homes burnt, and they themselves either murdered or taken into captivity.

Nor is the conduct of hostile parties, civil or eccclesiastical, more restrained by the power of conscience than that of hostile nations to one another. The laws of faction pay even less regard to the rules of justice than the laws of nations do. Though it has never been doubted whether faith ought to be kept with public enemies, it has often been furiously debated whether faith ought to be kept with rebels and heretics. Yet rebels and heretics are only those who, when things have come to a certain degree of violence, have the misfortune to belong to the weaker party. The impartial spectator is never at a greater distance than amidst the rage and violence of contending parties. For them it may be said that " such a spectator scarce exists anywhere in the universe. Even to the great judge of the universe they impute all their own prejudices, and often view that Divine Being as animated by all their own vindictive and implacable passions." Those who might act as the real controllers of such passions are too few to have any influence, being excluded by their own candour from the confidence of either party, and on that account condemned to be the weakest, though they may be the wisest men of their community. For " a true party man hates and despises candour ; and in reality there is no vice which could so effectually disqualify him for the trade of a party man as that single virtue."

But even when the real and impartial spectator is not at a great distance, but close at hand, our own selfish passions may be so strong as entirely to distort the judgment of the " man within the breast." We endeavour to view our own conduct in the light in which the impartial spectator would view it, both when we are about to act and when we have acted. On both occasions our views are apt to be partial, but they are more especially partial when it is most important that they should be otherwise.

This is the explanation of the moral phenomenon of self-deceit, and accounts for the otherwise remarkable fact, that our conscience in spite of its great authority and the great sanctions by which its voice is enforced, is so often prevented from acting with efficacy. When we are about to act, the eagerness of passion seldom allows us to consider what we are doing with the candour of an indifferent person. Our view of things is discoloured, even when we try to place ourselves in the situation of another and to regard our own interests from his point of view. We are constantly forced back by the fury of our passions to our own position, where everything seems magnified and misrepresented by self-love, whilst we catch but momentary glimpses of the view of the impartial spectator.

When we have acted, we can indeed enter more coolly into the sentiments of the indifferent spectator, and regard our own actions with his impartiality. We are then able to identify ourselves with the ideal man within the breast and view in our own character our own conduct and situation with the severe eyes of the most impartial spectator. But even our judgment is seldom quite candid. It is so disagreeable to think ill of ourselves, that we often purposely turn away our view from those circumstances which might render our judgment unfavourable. Rather than see our own behaviour in a disagreeable light, we often endeavour to exasperate anew those unjust passions which at first misled us; we awaken artificially our old hatreds and irritate afresh our almost forgotten resentments; and we thus persevere in injustice merely because we were unjust, and because we are ashamed and afraid to see that we were so.

And this partiality of mankind with regard to the propriety of their own conduct, both at the time of action and after it, is, our author thinks, one of the chief objections to the hypo-

thesis of the existence of a moral sense, and consequently an
additional argument in favour of his own theory of the phenomena of self-approbation. If it was by a peculiar faculty, like
the moral sense, that men judged of their own conduct—if
they were endowed with a particular power of perception
which distinguished the beauty and deformity of passions and
affections—surely this faculty would judge with more accuracy
concerning their own passions, which are more nearly exposed
to their view, than concerning those of other men, which are
necessarily of more distant observation. But it is notorious
that men generally judge more justly of others than they ever
do about themselves.

CHAPTER VII.

THEORY OF MORAL PRINCIPLES.

CLOSELY connected in Adam Smith's theory with his account of the growth of conscience is his account of the growth of those general moral principles we find current in the world. He regards these as a provision of Nature on our behalf, intended to counteract the perverting influences of self-love and the fatal weakness of self-deceit. They arise in the following way.

Continual observations on the conduct of others lead us gradually to form to ourselves certain general rules as to what it is fit and proper to do or to avoid. If some of their actions shock all our natural sentiments, and we hear other people express like detestation of them, we are then satisfied that we view them aright. We resolve therefore never to be guilty of the like offences, nor to make ourselves the objects of the general disapprobation they incur. Thus we arrive at a general rule, that all such actions are to be avoided, as tending to make us odious, contemptible, or punishable. Other actions, on the contrary, call forth our approbation, and the expressions of the same approval by others confirm us in the justice of our opinion. The eagerness of everybody to honour and reward them excite in us all those sentiments for which we have by nature the strongest desire—the love, the gratitude, the admiration of mankind. We thus become ambitious of performing the like, and thereby arrive at another general rule, that all such actions are good for us to do.

These general rules of morality, therefore, are ultimately founded on experience of what, in particular instances, our moral faculties approve of or condemn. They are not moral intuitions, or major premisses of conduct supplied to us by nature. We do not start with a general rule, and approve or disapprove of particular actions according as they conform or not to this general rule, but we form the general rule from experience of the approval or disapproval bestowed on particular actions. At the first sight of an inhuman murder, detestation of the crime would arise, irrespective of a reflection, that one of the most sacred rules of conduct prohibited the taking away another man's life, that this particular murder was a violation of that rule, and consequently that it was blameworthy. The detestation would arise instantaneously, and antecedent to our formation of any such general rule. The general rule would be formed afterwards upon the detestation we felt at such an action, at the thought of this and every other particular action of the same kind.

So when we read in history or elsewhere of either generous or base actions, our admiration for the one and our contempt for the other does not arise from the consideration that there are certain general rules which declare all actions of the one kind admirable and all of the other contemptible. Those rules are all formed from our experience of the effects naturally produced on us by all actions of one kind or the other.

Again, an amiable, a respectable, or a horrible action naturally excites for the person who performs them the love, the respect, or the horror of the spectator. The general rules, which determine what actions are or are not the objects of those different sentiments, can only be formed by observing what actions severally excite them.

When once these moral principles, or general rules, have been formed, and established by the concurrent voice of all mankind, they are often appealed to as the standards of judgment, when we seek to apportion their due degree of praise or blame to particular actions. From their being cited on all such occasions as the ultimate foundations of what is just and unjust, many eminent authors have been misled, and have drawn up their systems as if they supposed " that the original judgments of mankind, with regard to right and wrong, were formed, like the decisions of a court of judicatory, by considering first the general rule, and then, secondly, whether the particular action under consideration fell properly within its comprehension."

To pass now from the formation of such general rules to their function in practical ethics. They are most useful in correcting the misrepresentations of things which self-love is ever ready to suggest to us. Though founded on experience, they are none the less girt round with a sacred and unimpeachable authority. Take a man inclined to furious resentment, and ready to think that the death of his enemy is a small compensation for his provocation. From his observations on the conduct of others he has learned how horrible such revenges always appear, and has formed to himself a general rule, to abstain from them on all occasions. This rule preserves its authority with him under his temptation, when he might otherwise believe that his fury was just, and such as every impartial spectator would approve. The reverence for the rule, impressed upon him by past experience, checks the impetuosity of his passion, and helps him to correct the too partial views which self-love might suggest as proper in his situation. Even should he after all give way to his passion, he is terrified, at the moment of so doing, by the thought that he is violating a rule which he has never seen infringed with-

out the strongest expressions of disapprobation, or the evil
consequences of punishment.

That sense of duty, that feeling of the obligatoriness of the
rules of morality, which is so important a principle in human
life, and the only principle capable of governing the bulk of
mankind, is none other than an acquired reverence for these
general principles of conduct, arrived at in the manner described. This acquired reverence often serves as a substitute
for the sense of the propriety or impropriety of a particular
course of conduct. For many men live through their lives
without ever incurring much blame, who yet may never feel
the sentiment upon which our approbation of their conduct is
founded, but act merely from a regard for what they see are
the established rules of behaviour. For instance, a man who
has received great benefits from another may feel very little
gratitude in his heart, and yet act in every way as if he did
so, without any selfish or blameable motive, but simply from
reverence for the established rule of duty. Or a wife, who
may not feel any tender regard for her husband, may also act
as if she did, from mere regard to a sense of the duty of such
conduct. And though such a friend or such a wife are doubt-
less not the best of their kind, they are perhaps the second
best, and will be restrained from any decided dereliction from
their duty. Though "the coarse clay of which the bulk of
mankind are formed, cannot be wrought to such perfection"
as to act on all occasions with the most delicate propriety,
there is scarcely anybody who may not by education, discipline, and example, be so impressed with a regard to general
rules of conduct, as to act nearly always with tolerable decency,
and to avoid through the whole of his life any considerable
degree of blame.

Were it not indeed for this sense of duty, this sacred regard
for general rules, there is no one on whose conduct much reli-

ance could be placed. The difference between a man of principle and a worthless fellow is chiefly the difference between a man who adheres resolutely to his maxims of conduct and the man who acts "variously and accidentally as humour, inclination, or interest chance to be uppermost." Even the duties of ordinary politeness, which are not difficult to observe, depend very often for their observance more on regard for the general rule than on the actual feeling of the moment; and if these slight duties would, without such regard, be so readily violated, how slight, without a similar regard, would be the observance of the duties of justice, truth, fidelity, and chastity, for the violation of which so many strong motives might exist, and on the tolerable keeping of which the very existence of human society depends!

The obligatoriness of the rules of morality being thus first impressed upon us by nature, and afterwards confirmed by reasoning and philosophy, comes to be still further enhanced by the consideration that the said rules are the laws of God, who will reward or punish their observance or violation.

For whatever theory we may prefer of the origin of our moral faculties, there can be no doubt, Adam Smith argues, but "that they were given us for the direction of our conduct in this life." Our moral faculties "carry along with them the most evident badges of this authority, which denote that they were set up within us to be the supreme arbiters of all our actions, to superintend all our senses, passions, and appetites, and to judge how far each of them was either to be indulged or restrained." Our moral faculties are not on a level in this respect with the other faculties and appetites of our nature, for no other faculty or principle of action judges of any other. Love, for instance, does not judge of love, nor resentment of resentment. These two passions may be opposite to one another, but they do not approve or disapprove of

one another. It belongs to our moral faculties to judge
in this way of the other principles of our nature. What is
agreeable to our moral faculties is fit, and right, and proper
to be done; what is disagreeable to them is the contrary.
The sentiments which they approve of are graceful and becoming; the contrary ungraceful and unbecoming. The very
words—right, wrong, fit, improper, graceful, unbecoming—
mean only what pleases or displeases our moral faculties."

Since, then, they "were plainly intended to be the governing
principles of human nature, the rules which they prescribe are
to be regarded as the commands and laws of the Deity, pro-
mulgated by those vicegerents which He has thus set up
within us." These "vicegerents of God within us" never
fail to punish the violation of the rules of morality by the
torments of inward shame and self-condemnation, whilst they
always reward obedience to them with tranquillity and self-
satisfaction.

Having thus added the force of a religious sanction to the
authority of moral rules, and accounted for the feeling of
obligation in morality, from the physical basis of the pain or
pleasure of an instinctive antipathy or sympathy, the philosopher arrives at the question, How far our actions ought to
arise chiefly or entirely from a sense of duty or a regard to
general rules, and how far any other sentiment ought to
concur and have a principal influence. If a mere regard for
duty is the motive of most men, how far may their conduct
be regarded as right?

The answer to this question depends on two circumstances,
which may be considered in succession.

First, it depends on the natural agreeableness or deformity
of the affection of the mind which prompts us to any action,
whether the action should proceed rather from that affection
than from a regard to the general rule. Actions to which the

social or benevolent affections prompt us should proceed as much from the affections or passions themselves as from any regard to the general rules of conduct. To repay a kindness from a cold sense of duty, and from no personal affection to one's benefactor, is scarcely pleasing to the latter. As a father may justly complain of a son, who, though he fail in none of the offices of filial duty, yet manifests no affectionate reverence for his parent, so a son expects from his father something more than the mere performance of the duties of his situation.

The contrary maxim applies to the malevolent and unsocial passions. If we ought to reward, from gratitude and generosity, without any reflections on the propriety of rewarding, we ought always to punish with reluctance, and more from a sense of the propriety of punishing than from a mere disposition to revenge.

Where the selfish passions are concerned, we should attend to general rules in the pursuit of the lesser objects of private interest, but feel more passion for the objects themselves when they are of transcendent importance to us. The parsimony, for instance, of a tradesman should not proceed from a desire of the particular threepence he will save by it to-day, nor his attendance in his shop from a passion for the particular tenpence he will gain by it, but from a regard to the general rule which prescribes severe economy as the guiding principle of his life. To be anxious, or to lay a plot to gain or save a single shilling, would degrade him in the eyes of all his neighbours. But the more important objects of self-interest should be pursued with more concern for the things themselves and for their own sake; and a man would justly be regarded as mean-spirited who cared nothing about his election to Parliament or about the conquest of a province.

Secondly, it depends upon the exactness or inexactness of

the general rules themselves, how far our conduct ought to proceed entirely from a regard to them.

The general rules of almost all the virtues, which determine what are the duties of prudence, charity, generosity, gratitude, or friendship, admit of so many modifications and exceptions, that it is hardly possible to regulate our conduct entirely from regard to them. Even the rule of gratitude, plain as it seems to be, that it behoves us to make a return of equal, or, if possible, superior value to the benefit received from another, gives rise to numberless questions, whenever we seek to apply it to particular cases. For instance, if your friend lent you money in your distress, ought you to lend him money in his? and, if so, how much? and when? and for how long a time? No definite answer can be given to such questions. And even still more vague are the rules which indicate the duties of friendship, hospitality, humanity, and generosity.

Justice, indeed, is the only virtue of which the general rules determine exactly every external action required by it. If, for instance, you owe a man ten pounds, justice requires that you should pay him precisely that sum. The whole nature of your action is prescribed and fixed. The most sacred regard, therefore, is due to the rules of justice, and the actions it requires are never more properly performed than from a regard to the general rules themselves. In the practice of the other virtues, our conduct should be directed rather by a certain idea of propriety, by a certain taste for a particular kind of behaviour, than by any regard to a precise rule or maxim ; and we should consider more the end and foundation of the rule than the rule itself. But it is otherwise with justice, where we should attend more to the rule itself than to its end. Though the end of the rules of justice is to hinder us from hurting our neighbour, it would still be a crime to violate them, although we might pretend, with some show of reason, that this particular violation could do him no harm.

The rules of justice, and those of the other virtues, may therefore be compared in this way. The rules of justice are like the rules of grammar, those of the other virtues like the rules laid down by critics for the attainment of elegance in composition. Whilst the former are precise and accurate, the latter are vague and indeterminate, and present us rather with a general idea of perfection to be aimed at than any certain directions for acquiring it. As a man may be taught to write grammatically by rule, so perhaps may he be taught to act justly. But as there are no rules which will lead a man infallibly to elegance in composition, so there are none by which we can be taught to act on all occasions with prudence, magnanimity, or beneficence.

Lastly, in reference to moral principles, may be considered the case of their liability to perversion by a mistaken idea of them. There may be a most earnest desire so to act as to deserve approbation, and yet an erroneous conscience or a wrong sense of duty may lead to a course of conduct with which it is impossible for mankind to sympathize. "False notions of religion are almost the only causes which can occasion any very gross perversion of our natural sentiments in this way; and that principle which gives the greatest authority to the rules of duty, is alone capable of distorting them in any considerable degree. In all other cases common sense is sufficient to direct us, if not to the most exquisite propriety of conduct, yet to something which is not very far from it; and, provided we are desirous in earnest to do well, our behaviour will always, upon the whole, be praiseworthy." All men are agreed that the first rule of duty is to obey the will of God, but it is concerning the particular commandments imposed by that will that they differ so widely;

and crimes committed from a sense of religious duty are not
regarded with the indignation felt for ordinary crimes. The
sorrow we feel for Seid and Palmira in Voltaire's play of
Mahomet, when they are driven by a sense of religious duty to
murder an old man whom they honoured and esteemed, is the
same sorrow that we should feel for all men in a similar way
misled by religion.

CHAPTER VIII.

THE RELATION OF RELIGION TO MORALITY.

THE relation which, in Adam Smith's system, religion bears to ethics has been already indicated in the last chapter. Although he regards morality as quite independent of religion, as intelligible and possible without it, religion nevertheless stands out visibly in the background of his theory, and is appealed to as a strong support of virtuous conduct, and as lending additional sanctity to the authority of moral rules.

These moral rules, though sufficiently sanctioned by the same feelings of human approbation or disapprobation which originally gave rise to them, derive an additional sanction rom natural religion. It was too important for the happiness of mankind, that the natural sense of duty should thus be enforced by the terrors of religion, "for nature to leave it dependent upon the slowness and uncertainty of philosophical researches."

This identification therefore of the rules of morality with the rules of religion was first impressed upon mankind by nature, and then afterwards confirmed by philosophy. Naturally led as men everywhere are, and were, to ascribe to those beings, which in any country happen to be the objects of religious fear, all their own sentiments and passions, it could not but arise, that as they ascribed to them those passions which do least honour to our own species—such as lust, avarice, envy, or revenge—they should also ascribe to

them those qualities which are the great ornaments of
humanity—the love of virtue and beneficence, and the hatred
of vice and injustice. The injured man would call on Jupiter
to witness his wrong, never doubting but that it would be
beheld by him with the same indignation that would actuate
the meanest of mankind against it; whilst the man, who did
the wrong, transferred to the same omnipresent and irresistible
being the resentment he was also conscious of in mankind.
"These natural hopes, and fears, and suspicions, were pro-
pagated by sympathy, and confirmed by education; and the
gods were universally represented and believed to be the
rewarders of humanity and mercy, and the avengers of perfidy
and injustice. And thus religion, even in its rudest form,
gave a sanction to the rules of morality, long before the age
of artificial reasoning and philosophy."

Reasoning, when applied, confirmed the original antici-
pations of nature. For from the recognition of the fact,
already noticed, that our moral faculties were *intended* to be
the governing principles of our nature, it became clear that
the rules they formulated, in compliance with such an intention, might be regarded as the laws of the Deity, who set
up those moral faculties as His " vicegerents within us."

Another consideration confirms this reasoning. As by
obeying the rules prescribed to us by our moral faculties, we
pursue the most effectual means for promoting the happiness
of mankind, and as the happiness of mankind seems to be the
original purpose intended by the Author of Nature, it is
evident that by obeying the moral rules we in some sense co-
operate with the Deity, and advance, as far as is in our
power, the plan of Providence. As also by acting otherwise
we obstruct in some measure His scheme, we declare ourselves
in some measure the enemies of God, so we are naturally
encouraged to look for His favour and reward in the one

case, and to dread His vengeance and punishment in the other.

Moreover, although virtue and vice, as far as they can be either rewarded or punished by the sentiments and opinions of mankind, meet even here, according to the common course of things, with their deserts, we are compelled by the best principles of our nature, by our love of virtue and our abhorrence of vice and injustice, to look to a future life for the rectification of occasional results of virtue or vice which shock all our natural sentiments of justice. The indignation we feel when we see violence and artifice prevail over sincerity and justice, the sorrow we feel for the sufferings of the innocent, the resentment we feel and often cannot satisfy against the oppressor, all prompt us to hope "that the great Author of our nature will Himself execute hereafter, what all the principles which He has given us for the direction of our conduct prompt us to attempt even here; that He will complete the plan which He Himself has thus taught us to begin; and will, in a life to come, render to every one according to the works which he has performed in this world."

When, therefore, the general rules of morality which determine the merit or demerit of actions come thus to be regarded, says Adam Smith, as the laws of an all-powerful Being, who watches over our conduct, and who, in a life to come, will reward the observance and punish the breach of them, they necessarily acquire a new sacredness. The sense of propriety, which dictates obedience to the will of the Deity as the supreme rule of our conduct, is confirmed by the strongest motives of self-interest. For it is an idea, well capable of restraining the most headstrong passions, that however much we may escape the observation or the punishment of mankind, we can never escape the observation nor the punishment of God.

It is on account of the additional sanction which religion thus confers upon the rules of morality that so great confidence is generally placed in the probity of those who seem deeply impressed with a sense of religion. They seem to act under an additional tie to those which regulate the conduct of others. For regard to the propriety of action and to reputation, regard to the applause of his own breast as well as to that of others, are motives which have the same influence over the religious man as over the man of the world; but the former acts under another restraint, that of future recompense, and accordingly greater trust is reposed in his conduct.

Nor is this greater trust unreasonably placed in him. For "wherever the natural principles of religion are not corrupted by the factious and party zeal of some worthless cabal; wherever the first duty which it requires is to fulfil all the obligations of morality; wherever men are not taught to regard frivolous observances as more immediate duties of religion than acts of justice and beneficence; and to imagine, that by sacrifices, and ceremonies, and vain supplications, they can bargain with the Deity for fraud, and perfidy, and violence, the world undoubtedly judges right in this respect, and justly places a double confidence in the rectitude of the religious man's behaviour."

At the same time Adam Smith resents strongly the doctrine that religious principles are the only laudable motives of action, the doctrine, "that we ought neither to reward from gratitude nor punish from resentment, that we ought neither to protect the helplessness of our children, nor afford support to the infirmities of our parents, from natural affection; but that we ought to do all things from the love of the Deity, and from a desire only to render ourselves agreeable to Him, and to direct our conduct according to His will." It should not

be the sole motive and principle of our conduct in the performance of our various duties that God has commanded us
to perform them, though that it should be our ruling and
governing principle is the precept of philosophy and common
sense no less than it is of Christianity.

In the same way that Adam Smith regards religion as an
additional sanction to the natural rules of morality, does
he regard it as the only effectual consolation in the case of a
man unjustly condemned by the world for a crime of which
he is innocent. To such an one, that humble philosophy
which confines its view to this life can afford but little comfort. Deprived of everything that could make either life or
death respectable, condemned to death and to everlasting
infamy, the view of another world, where his innocence will be
declared and his virtue rewarded, can alone compensate him
for the misery of his situation.

"Our happiness in this life is thus, upon many occasions,
dependent upon the humble hope and expectation of a life to
come—a hope and expectation deeply rooted in human nature,
which can alone support its lofty ideas of its own dignity, can
alone illumine the dreary prospect of its continually approaching mortality, and maintain its cheerfulness under all the
heaviest calamities to which, from the disorders of this life,
it may sometimes be exposed. That there is a world to come,
where exact justice will be done to every man . . . . . is a
doctrine, in every respect so venerable, so comfortable to the
weakness, so flattering to the grandeur of human nature, that
the virtuous man who has the misfortune to doubt of it cannot possibly avoid wishing most earnestly and anxiously to
believe it."

This doctrine, Adam Smith thinks, could never have fallen
into disrepute, had not a doctrine been asserted of a future
distribution of rewards and punishments, at total variance with

all our moral sentiments. The preference of assiduous flattery to merit or service, which is regarded as the greatest reproach even to the weakness of earthly sovereigns, is often ascribed to divine perfection; "and the duties of devotion, the public and private worship of the Deity, have been represented, even by men of virtue and abilities, as the sole virtues which can either entitle to reward, or exempt from punishment, in the life to come."

There is the same absurdity in the notion, which had even its advocate in a philosopher like Massillon, that one hour or day spent in the mortifications of a monastery has more merit in the eye of God than a whole life spent honourably in the profession of a soldier. Such a doctrine is surely contrary to all our moral sentiments, and the principles by which we have been taught by nature to regulate our admiration or contempt. " It is this spirit, however, which, while it has reserved the celestial regions for monks and friars, or for those whose conduct or conversation resembled those of monks and friars, has condemned to the infernal all the heroes, all the statesmen and lawyers, all the poets and philosophers of former ages; all those who have invented, improved, or excelled in the arts which contribute to the subsistence, to the conveniency, or to the ornament of life; all the great protectors, instructors, and benefactors of mankind; all those to whom our natural sense of praiseworthiness forces us to ascribe the highest merit and the most exalted virtue. Can we wonder that so strange an application of this most respectable doctrine should sometimes have exposed it to derision and contempt?"

Although, then, Adam Smith considers that reason corroborates the teaching of natural religion regarding the existence of God and the life hereafter, he nowhere recognizes any moral obligation in the belief of one or the other; and they occupy in his system a very similar position to that which they occupy in Kant's, who treats the belief in the existence of God and in immortality as Postulates of the Practical Reason, that is to say, as assumptions *morally* necessary, however incapable of speculative proof. Adam Smith, however, does not approach either subject at all from the speculative side, but confines himself entirely to the moral basis of both, to the arguments in their favour which the moral phenomena of life afford, such as have been already indicated.

But besides the argument in favour of the existence of God derived from our moral sentiments, the only argument he employs is derived, not from the logical inconceivability of a contrary belief, but from the incompatibility of such a contrary belief with the happiness of the man so believing. A man of universal benevolence or boundless goodwill can enjoy no solid happiness unless he is convinced that all the inhabitants of the universe are under the immediate care of that all-wise Being, who directs all the movements of nature, and who is compelled, by His own unalterable perfections, to maintain in it at all times the greatest possible quantity of happiness. To a man of universal benevolence, " the very suspicion of a fatherless world must be the most melancholy of all reflections ; from the thought that all the unknown regions of infinite and incomprehensible space may be filled with nothing but endless misery and wretchedness. All the splendour of the highest prosperity can never enlighten the gloom with which so dreadful an idea must necessarily overshadow the imagination ; nor, in a wise and virtuous man, can all the sorrow of the most afflicting adversity ever dry up the joy which necessarily springs from the habitual and thorough conviction of the truth of the contrary system."

It was a well-known doctrine of the Stoic philosophy, that

a man should resign all his wishes and interests with perfect
confidence to the benevolent wisdom which directs the universe,
and should seek his happiness chiefly in the contemplation of
the perfection of the universal system. With this conception
of resignation Adam Smith very closely agrees, in his description of the sentiments which become the wise and virtuous
man with regard to his relation to the great sum of things.
Just as he should be willing to sacrifice his own interest to
that of his own order, and that of his own order again to
that of his country, so he should be willing to sacrifice all
those inferior interests "to the greater interest of the universe,
to the interest of that great society of all sensible and intelligent beings, of which God Himself is the immediate ad-
ministrator and director. If he is deeply impressed with the
habitual and thorough conviction that this benevolent and
all-wise Being can admit into the system of His government
no partial evil which is not necessary for the universal good,
he must consider all the misfortunes which may befall himself, his friends, his society, or his country, as necessary for
the prosperity of the universe, and therefore as what he
ought not only to submit to with resignation, but as what
he himself, if he had known all the connexions and depen-
dencies of things, ought sincerely and devoutly to have wished
for."

A wise man should be capable of doing what a good soldier
is always ready to do. For the latter, when ordered by his
general, will march with alacrity to the forlorn station, knowing
that he would not have been sent there but for the safety of
the whole army and the success of the war, and he will cheer-
fully sacrifice his own little system to the welfare of a greater.
But "no conductor of an army can deserve more unlimited
trust, more ardent and zealous affection, than the great Conductor of the universe. In the greatest public as well as
private disasters, a wise man ought to consider that he himself,

his friends and countrymen, have only been ordered upon the forlorn station of the universe; that had it not been necessary for the good of the whole, they would not have been so ordered; and that it is their duty, not only with humble resignation to submit to this allotment, but to endeavour to embrace it with alacrity and joy."

To the question, how far a man should seek his highest happiness in the contemplation of the system of the universe; or, in other words, whether the contemplative or the practical life is the higher and better, Adam Smith replies hesitatingly in favour of the latter. The most sublime object of human contemplation is "the idea of that Divine Being, whose benevolence and wisdom have from all eternity contrived and conducted the immense machine of the universe, so as at all times to produce the greatest possible quantity of happiness." A man believed to be chiefly occupied in this sublime contemplation seldom fails of the highest veneration; and even though his life should be altogether contemplative, is often regarded with a sort of religious respect far higher than is generally bestowed on the most useful and active citizen. Marcus Antoninus has, perhaps, received more admiration for his meditations on this subject than for all the different transactions of his just and beneficent reign.

Nevertheless, the care of the universe not being the concern of man, but only the care of his own happiness, or that of his family, friends, or country, he can never be justified in neglecting the more humble department of affairs because he is engaged in the contemplation of the higher. He must not lay himself open to the charge which was brought against Marcus Antoninus, that whilst he was occupied in contemplating the prosperity of the universe he neglected that of the Roman empire. "The most sublime speculation of the contemplative philosopher can scarce compensate the neglect of the smallest active duty."

CHAPTER IX.

THE science of ethics, according to Adam Smith, deals mainly with two principal questions, the first concerning the nature of moral approbation, or the origin of our feelings of right and wrong, and the second concerning the nature of virtue, or the moral elements of which virtue consists. The first question is that to which the answer has already been given; the second question to which the answer yet remains to be given, is "What is the tone of temper, and tenor of conduct, which constitutes the excellent and praiseworthy character, the character which is the natural object of esteem, honour, and approbation?" Does virtue consist in benevolence, as some have maintained, or is it but a form of self-love, as others have maintained; or does it consist in some relation of the benevolent and selfish affections to one another?

The general answer which Adam Smith makes to this question is, that virtue consists in a certain relation to one another of our selfish and unselfish affections, not exclusively in a predominance of either of them. "The man of the most perfect virtue," he says, "the man whom we naturally love and revere the most, is he who joins, to the most perfect command of his own original and selfish feelings, the most exquisite sensibility both to the original and sympathetic feelings of others." It is the man who unites the gentler virtues of humanity and sensibility with the severer virtues of self-control and self-denial. "To feel much for others, and little for ourselves, to restrain

our selfish, and to indulge our benevolent affections, constitutes the perfection of humanity."

Consequently any man's character for virtue must depend
upon those two different aspects of his conduct which regard
both himself and others ; and a character completely virtuous
will consist in a combination of those qualities which have a
beneficial effect alike on an individual's own happiness as on
that of his fellow-men. These qualities are Prudence, Justice
and Beneficence; and " the man who acts according to the
rules of perfect prudence, of strict justice, and of proper
benevolence, may be said to be perfectly virtuous."

1. The quality of Prudence is that side of a man's character
which concerns only his own happiness, and it has for its
object the care of his personal health, fortune, rank, and reputation. The first lessons in this virtue are taught us " by the
voice of nature herself," who directs us by the appetites of
hunger and thirst, and by agreeable or disagreeable sensations,
to provide for our bodily preservation and health. As we
grow older we learn that only by proper care and foresight
with respect to our external fortune can we ensure the means
of satisfying our natural appetites, and we are further led to
a desire of the advantages of fortune by experience that
chiefly on their possession or supposed possession depends
that credit and rank among our equals which is perhaps the
strongest of all our desires. Security therefore of health,
fortune, and rank, constitutes the principal object of Prudence.

This outline of the subject-matter of Prudence, Adam
Smith proceeds to fill up with a sketch of the character of the
Prudent Man, which modelled, as it appears to be, on
Aristotle's delineation of imaginary types of the different
virtues, is so characteristic an illustration of our author's style
and thought, that it is best presented to the reader in the
following extracts from the original :—

" The prudent man always studies seriously and earnestly to understand whatever he professes to understand and not merely to persuade other people that he understands it; and though his talents may not always be very brilliant, they are always perfectly genuine. He neither endeavours to impose upon you by the cunning devices of an artful impostor, nor by the arrogant airs of an assuming pedant, nor by the confident assertions of a superficial and impudent pretender; he is not ostentatious even of the abilities he really possesses. His conversation is simple and modest, and he is averse to all the quackish arts by which other people so frequently thrust themselves into public notice. . . . .

" The prudent man is always sincere, and feels horror at the very thought of exposing himself to the disgrace which attends upon the detection of falsehood. But though always sincere, he is not always frank and open; and though he never tells anything but the truth, he does not always think himself bound, when not properly called upon, to tell the whole truth. As he is cautious in his actions, so he is reserved in his speech, and never rashly or unnecessarily obtrudes his opinion concerning either things or persons.

" The prudent man, though not always distinguished by the most exquisite sensibility, is always very capable of friendship. But his friendship is not that ardent and passionate but too often transitory affection which appears so delicious to the generosity of youth and inexperience. It is a sedate, but steady and faithful attachment to a few well-chosen companions; in the choice of whom he is not guided by the giddy admiration of shining accomplishments, but by the sober esteem of modesty, discretion, and good conduct. But though capable of friendship, he is not always much disposed to general sociality. He rarely frequents, and more rarely figures in, those convivial societies which are distinguished for

the jollity and gaiety of their conversation. Their way of
life might too often interfere with the regularity of his temperance, might interrupt the steadiness of his industry, or break
in upon the strictness of his frugality.

"But though his conversation may not always be very
sprightly or diverting, it is always perfectly inoffensive. He
hates the thought of being guilty of any petulance or rudeness; he never assumes impertinently over anybody, and
upon all occasions is willing to place himself rather below than
above his equals. Both in his conduct and conversation he is
an exact observer of decency, and respects with an almost
religious scrupulosity all the established decorums and cere-
monials of society. . . . .

"The man who lives within his income is naturally contented with his situation, which by continual though small
accumulations is growing better and better every day. He is
enabled gradually to relax both in the rigour of his parsimony
and in the severity of his application; . . . He has no
anxiety to change so comfortable a situation, and does not go
in quest of new enterprises and adventures which might
endanger, but could not well increase, the secure tranquillity
which he actually enjoys. If he enters into any new projects,
they are likely to be well concerted and well prepared. He
can never be hurried or driven into them by any necessity,
but has always time and leisure to deliberate soberly and
coolly concerning what are likely to be their consequences.

"The prudent man is not willing to subject himself to any
responsibility which his duty does not impose upon him. He
is not a bustler in business where he has no concern; is not a
meddler in other people's affairs; is not a professed counsellor
or adviser, who obtrudes his advice where nobody is asking it;
he confines himself as much as his duty will permit to his own
affairs, and has no taste for that foolish importance which

many people wish to derive from appearing to have some influence in the management of those of other people; he is averse to enter into any party disputes, hates faction, and is not always very forward to listen to the voice even of noble and great ambition. When distinctly called upon he will not decline the service of his country; but he will not cabal in order to force himself into it, and would be much better pleased that the public business were well managed by some other person than that he himself should have the trouble and incur the responsibility of managing it. In the bottom of his heart he would prefer the undisturbed enjoyment of secure tranquillity, not only to all the vain splendour of successful ambition, but to the real and solid glory of performing the greatest and most magnanimous actions."

Such is Adam Smith's account of the character of the Prudent Man, a character which he himself admits commands rather a cold esteem than any very ardent love or admiration. He distinguishes it from that higher form of prudence which belongs to the great general, statesman, or legislator, and which is the application of wise and judicious conduct to greater and nobler purposes than the mere objects of personal interest. This superior prudence necessarily supposes the utmost perfection of all the intellectual and all the moral virtues; it is the most perfect wisdom combined with the most perfect virtue; it is the best head joined to the best heart.

2. Justice and Benevolence—the disposition either to refrain from injuring our neighbour, or else to benefit him—are the two qualities of a virtuous character which affect the happiness of other people. A sacred and religious regard not to hurt or disturb the happiness of others, even in cases where no law can protect them, constitutes the character of the perfectly innocent and just man, and is a character which can scarcely fail to be accompanied by many other virtues, such

as great feeling for others, great humanity, and great benevolence. But whilst benevolence is a positive moral factor,
justice is only a negative one; benevolence, therefore, requires
the greater consideration of the two.

3. Benevolence comprises all the good offices which we owe
to our family, our friends, our country, and our fellow-
creatures. This is the order in which the world is recommended to our beneficent affections by Nature, who has
strictly proportioned the strength of our benevolence to the
degree in which it is necessary or likely to be useful.

Thus every man is first and principally recommended to
his own care, being better able to take care of himself than
of any other person. After himself, the members of his own
family, those who usually live in the same house with him—
his parents, children, or brothers and sisters—are naturally the
objects of his warmest affections. The earliest friendships
are those among brothers and sisters, whose power for giving
pleasure or pain to one another renders their good agreement
so much the more necessary for the happiness of the family.
The sympathy between more distant relations, being less
necessary, is proportionately weaker.

Here, again, may be noticed the influence of custom over
our moral sentiments. Affection is really habitual sympathy;
and, from our general experience that the state of habitual
sympathy in which near relations stand to one another produces a certain affection between them, we expect always to
find such affection, and are shocked when we fail to do so.
Hence the general rule is established, from a great number of
instances, that persons related to one another in a certain
degree ought to be affected towards one another in a certain
manner, and that the highest impropriety exists in the absence
of any such affection between them.

This disposition to accommodate and assimilate our sentiments and principles to those of persons we live with or see often—a disposition which arises from the obvious convenience of such a general agreement—leads us to expect to find friendship subsisting between colleagues in office, partners in trade, or even between persons living in the same neighbourhood. There are certain small good offices which are universally regarded as due to a neighbour in preference to any other person; and a certain friendliness is expected of neighbours, from the mere fact of the sympathy naturally associated with living in the same locality.

But these sort of attachments, which the Romans expressed by the word *necessitudo,* as if to denote that they arose from the necessity of the situation, are inferior to those friendships which are founded not merely on a sympathy, rendered habitual for the sake of convenience, but on a natural sympathy and approbation of a man's good conduct. Such friendship can subsist only among the good. " Men of virtue only can feel that entire confidence in the conduct and behaviour of one another, which can at all times assure them that they can never either offend or be offended by one another. Vice is always capricious, virtue only is regular and orderly. The attachment which is founded upon the love of virtue, as it is certainly of all attachments the most virtuous, so it is likewise the happiest, as well as the most permanent and secure. Such friendships need not be confined to a single person, but may safely embrace all the wise and virtuous with whom we have been long and intimately acquainted, and upon whose wisdom and virtue we can, upon that account, entirely depend."

And the same principles which direct the order of our benevolent affections towards individuals, likewise direct their order towards societies, recommending to them before all others those to which they can be of most importance. Our

I

native country is the largest society upon which our good or
bad conduct can have much influence. It is that to which
alone our good-will can be directed with effect. Accordingly,
it is by nature most strongly recommended to us, as comprehending not only our own personal safety and prosperity, but
that of our children, our parents, our relations, and friends.
It is thus endeared to us by all our private benevolent, as well
as by our selfish affections. Hence its prosperity and glory
seem to reflect some sort of honour upon ourselves, and "when
we compare it with other societies of the same kind, we are
proud of its superiority, and mortified, in some degree, if it
appears in any respect below them."

But it is necessary to distinguish the love of our own
country from a foolish dislike to every other one. " The love
of our own nation often disposes us to view, with the most
malignant jealousy and envy, the prosperity and aggrandizement of any other neighbouring nation. Independent and
neighbouring nations, having no common superior to decide
their disputes, all live in continual dread and suspicion of one
another. Each sovereign, expecting little justice from his
neighbours, is disposed to treat them with as little as he
expects from them. The regard for the laws of nations, or
for those rules which independent states profess or pretend to
think themselves bound to observe in their dealings with one
another, is often very little more than mere pretence and profession. From the smallest interest, upon the slightest
provocation, we see those rules every day either evaded or
directly violated without shame or remorse. Each nation
foresees, or imagines it foresees, its own subjugation in the
increasing power and aggrandizement of any of its neighbours; and the mean principle of national prejudice is often
founded on the noble one of the love of our own country.
 . . . . France and England may each of them have some

reason to dread the increase of the naval and military power of the other; but for either of them to envy the internal happiness and prosperity of the other, the cultivation of its lands, the advancement of its manufactures, the increase of its commerce, the security and number of its ports and harbours, its proficiency in all the liberal arts and sciences, is surely beneath the dignity of two such great nations. These are the real improvements of the world we live in. Mankind are benefited, human nature is ennobled by them. In such improvements each nation ought not only to endeavour itself to excel, but, from the love of mankind, to promote, instead of obstructing, the excellence of its neighbours. These are all proper objects of national emulation, not of national prejudice or envy."

This passage is of interest as coming from the future author of the *Wealth of Nations*, the future founder of the doctrine of free trade; and of historical interest, as reflecting cultivated opinion at a time when England was just in the middle of the Seven years' war, is the remark that the most extensive public benevolence is that of the statesmen who project or form alliances between neighbouring or not very distant nations, "for the preservation either of what is called the balance of power, or of the general peace and tranquillity of the states within the circle of their negotiations."

But the ordinary love of our country involves two things : a certain reverence for the form of government actually established, and an earnest desire to render the condition of our fellow-citizens as safe, respectable, and happy, as possible. It is only in times of public discontent and faction that these two principles may draw different ways, and lead to doubt whether a change in the constitution might not be most conducive to the general happiness. In such times, the leaders of the discontented party often propose "to new-model the constitution, and to alter, in some of its most essential parts, that system of government under which the subjects of a great empire have enjoyed perhaps peace, security, and even glory, during the course of several centuries together." And it may require the highest effort of political wisdom to determine when a real patriot ought to support and try to re-establish the authority of the old system, and when he ought to give way to the more daring, but often dangerous, spirit of innovation.

Nothing, indeed, is more fatal to the good order of society than the policy of "a man of system," who is so enamoured of his own ideal plan of government as to be unable to suffer the smallest deviation from any part of it, and who insists upon establishing, and establishing all at once, and in spite of all opposition, whatever his idea may seem to require. Such a man erects his own judgment into the supreme standard of right and wrong, and fancies himself the only wise and worthy man in the commonwealth. "It is upon this account that of all political speculators sovereign princes are by far the most dangerous. This arrogance is perfectly familiar to them. They entertain no doubt of the immense superiority of their own judgment . . . . and consider the state as made for themselves, not themselves for the state."

It is otherwise with the real patriot, with the man whose public spirit is prompted altogether by humanity and benevolence. He "will respect the established powers and privileges even of individuals, and still more those of the great orders and societies into which the state is divided. Though he should consider some of them as in some measure abusive, he will content himself with moderating, what he often cannot annihilate without great violence. When he cannot conquer the rooted prejudices of the people by reason and persuasion, he will not attempt to subdue them by force, but will religiously observe what by Cicero is justly called the divine maxim of Plato, never to use violence to his country, no more than to his parents. He will accommodate, as well as he can, his public arrangements to the confirmed habits and prejudices of the people; and will remedy, as well as he can, the inconveniences which may flow from the want of those regulations which the people are adverse to submit to. When he cannot establish the right, he will not disdain to ameliorate the wrong; but, like Solon, where he cannot establish the best system of laws, he will endeavour to establish the best that the people can bear."

But although Prudence, Justice, and Benevolence comprise all the qualities and actions which go to make up the highest Virtue, another quality, that of Self-Command, is also necessary, in order that we may not be misled by our own passions to violate the rules of the other three virtues. The most perfect knowledge, unless supported by the most perfect self-command, will not of itself enable us to do our duty.

The two sets of passions which it is necessary to command are those which, like fear and anger, it is difficult to control even for a moment, or those which, like the love of ease, pleasure, applause, or other selfish gratifications, may be restrained indeed often for a moment, but often prevail in the long run, by reason of their continual solicitations. The command of the first set of passions constitutes what the ancient moralists denominated fortitude, or strength of mind; that of the other set what they called temperance, decency, moderation.

Self-command therefore is a union of the qualities of fortitude and temperance; and independently of the beauty it derives from utility, as enabling us to act according to the dictates of prudence, justice, and benevolence, it has a beauty of its own, and deserves for its own sake alone some degree of our admiration and esteem.

For self-command is not only itself a great virtue, but it is the chief source of the lustre of all the other virtues. Thus the character of the most exalted wisdom and virtue is that of a man who acts with the greatest coolness in extreme dangers and difficulties, who observes religiously the sacred rules of justice, in spite of the temptation by his strongest interests or by the grossest injuries to violate them, and who suffers not the benevolence of his temper to be damped by the ingratitude of its objects.

The first quality in the character of self-command is *Courage*, or the restraint of the passion of fear. The command of fear is more admirable than that of anger. The exertion displayed by a man, who in persecution or danger suffers no word or gesture to escape him, which does not perfectly accord with the feelings of the most indifferent spectator, commands a high degree of admiration. Had Socrates been suffered to die quietly in his bed, even his glory as a philosopher might never have attained that dazzling splendour which has ever been attached to him. Courage even causes some degree of regard to be paid to the greatest criminals who die with firmness; and the freedom from the fear of death, the great fear of all, is that which ennobles the profession of a soldier, and bestows upon it a rank and dignity superior to that of every other profession. It is for this reason that some sort of esteem is attached to characters, however worthless, who have conducted with success a great warlike exploit, though undertaken contrary to every principle of justice, and carried on with no regard to humanity.

The command of the passion of anger, though it has no special name like that of the passion of fear, merits on many occasions much admiration. But whilst courage is always admired irrespective of its motive, our approval of the command of anger depends on our sense of its dignity and propriety. Our whole sense of the beauty of the Philippics of Demosthenes or of the Catiline orations of Cicero is derived from the propriety with which a just indignation is expressed in them. This just indignation is nothing but anger restrained to that degree with which the impartial spectator can sympathize. It is because a blustering and noisy anger interests the spectator less for the angry man than for the person with whom he is angry that the nobleness of pardoning so often appears superior to the most perfect propriety of resentment. But the fact that the restraint of anger may be due to the presence of fear accounts for the less general admiration that is paid to the former than is often paid to the latter. The indulgence of anger seems to show a sort of courage and superiority to fear, and for that reason it is sometimes an object of vanity, whilst the indulgence of fear is never an object of a similar ostentation.

The next quality in Self-Command is *Temperance*, or the command of those less violent passions which appeal to our love of ease or pleasure. The command of these passions can seldom, like the command of anger or fear, be directed to any bad end. Temperance and moderation, which include such virtues as industry, frugality, or chastity, are always amiable; but inasmuch as their exercise requires a gentler though steadier exertion than is necessary for the restraint of anger or fear, the beauty and grace which belong to them are less dazzling, though none the less pleasing, than the qualities which attend the more splendid actions of the hero, the statesman, or the legislator.

It has already been observed that the point of propriety, or degree of any passion with which an impartial spectator can approve, is differently situated in different passions, in some cases lying nearer to the excess, and in others nearer to the defect. But it remains to be noticed, " that the passions which the spectator is most disposed to sympathize with, and in which, upon that account, the point of propriety may be said to stand high, are those of which the immediate feeling or sensation is more or less agreeable to the person principally concerned; and that, on the contrary, the passions which the spectator is least disposed to sympathize with, and in which, upon that account, the point of propriety may be said to stand low, are those of which the immediate feeling or sensation is more or less disagreeable or even painful to the person principally concerned."

For instance, the disposition to the social affections, to humanity, kindness, natural affection, or friendship, being always agreeable to the person who feels them, meets with more sympathy in its excess than in its defect. Though we blame a disposition, that is too ready and indiscriminate in its kindness, we regard it with pity rather than with the dislike which we feel towards a person who is defective in kindness, or characterized by what is called hardness of heart. On the other hand, the disposition to the unsocial affections— to anger, hatred, envy, or malice—as it is more agreeable to the person principally concerned in defect than in excess, so any defect of those passions approaches nearer to the point of propriety approved of by the spectator than any excess in their manifestation. Their excess renders a man wretched and miserable in his own mind, and hence their defect is more pleasing to others. Nevertheless even the defect may be excessive. The want of proper indignation is a most essential defect in any character, if it prevents a man from protecting either himself or his friends from insult or injustice. Or again, that defect of or freedom from envy, which, founded on indolence or good nature, or on an aversion to trouble or op-

position, suffers others readily to rise far above us, as it generally leads to much regret and repentance afterwards, so it
often gives place "to a most malignant envy in the end, and
to a hatred of that superiority which those who have once
attained it may often become really entitled to, by the very
circumstance of having attained it. In order to live com-
fortably in the world, it is upon all occasions as necessary to
defend our dignity and rank as it is to defend our lives or our
fortune."

Sensibility to our own personal dangers, injuries, or misfortunes, is more apt to offend by its excess than by its defect,
and here again the same rule prevails, for a fretful or timid
disposition renders a man miserable to himself as well as
offensive to others. A calm temper, which contentedly lays
its account to suffer somewhat from both the natural and
moral evils infesting the world, is a blessing to the man himself, and gives ease and security to all his fellows. But such
defect of sensibility may also be excessive, for the man who
feels little for his own misfortunes or injuries will always feel
less for those of other people, and be less disposed to relieve or
resent them.

A defect of sensibility to the pleasures and amusements of
life is more offensive than the excess, for both to the person
primarily affected and to the spectator a strong propensity to
joy is more pleasing than the contrary. This propensity is
only blamed when its indulgence is unsuited to time or place,
to the age or the situation of a person, and when it leads to
the neglect of his interest or duty. But it is rather in such
cases the weakness of the sense of propriety and duty that is
blamed than the strength of the propensity to joy.

Self-esteem also is more agreeable in excess than in defect,
for it is so much more pleasant to think highly than it is to
think meanly of ourselves. And just as we apply two different

standards to our judgment about others, so in self-estimation we apply to ourselves both the standard of absolute perfection and that of the ordinary approximation thereto. To these two standards the same man often bestows a different degree of attention at different times. In every man there exists an idea of exact propriety and perfection ; an idea gradually formed from observations of himself and others, "the slow, gradual, and progressive work of the great demigod within the breast, the great judge and arbiter of conduct." It is an idea which, in every man, is more or less accurately drawn, more or less justly coloured and designed, according to the delicacy and care with which the observations have been made.

But it is the wise and virtuous man who, having made these observations with the utmost care, directs his conduct chiefly by this ideal standard, and esteems himself rightly in consequence. He feels the imperfect success of all his best endeavours to assimilate his conduct to that archetype of perfection, and remembers with humiliation the frequency of his aberration from the exact rules of perfect propriety. And so conscious is he of his imperfection that, even when he judges himself by the second standard of ordinary rectitude, he is unable to regard with contempt the still greater imperfection of other people. Thus his character is one of real modesty, for he combines, with a very moderate estimate of his own merit, a full sense of the merit of others.

The difference indeed between such a man and the ordinary man is the difference between the great artist who judges of his own works by his conception of ideal perfection and the lesser artist who judges of his work merely by comparison with the work of other artists. The poet Boileau, who used to say that no great man was ever completely satisfied with his own work, being once assured by Santeuil, a writer of

Latin verses, that he, for his own part, was completely satisfied with *his* own, replied that he was certainly the only great man who ever was so. Yet how much harder of attainment is the ideal perfection in conduct than it is in art! For the artist may work undisturbed, and in full possession of all his skill and experience. But "the wise man must support the propriety of his own conduct in health and in sickness, in success and in disappointment, in the hour of fatigue and drowsy indolence, as well as in that of the most wakened attention. The most sudden and unexpected assaults of difficulty and distress must never surprise him. The injustice of other people must never provoke him to injustice. The violence of faction must never confound him. All the hardships and hazards of war must never either dishearten or appal him."

Pride and vanity are two distinct kinds of that excessive self-estimation which we blame in persons who enjoy no distinguished superiority over the common level of mankind; and though the proud man is often vain, and the vain man proud, the two characters are easily distinguishable.

The proud man is sincere, and in the bottom of his heart convinced of his own superiority. He wishes you to view him in no other light than that in which, when he places himself in your situation, he really views himself. He only demands justice. He deigns not to explain the grounds of his pretensions; he disdains to court esteem, and even affects to despise it. He is too well contented with himself to think that his character requires any amendment. He does not always feel at ease in the company of his equals, and still less in that of his superiors. Unable as he is to lay down his lofty pretensions, and overawed by such superiority, he has recourse to humbler company, for which he has little respect, and in which he finds little pleasure—that of his inferiors or dependants. If he visits his superiors, it is to show that he

is entitled to live with them more than from any real satisfaction he derives from them.   He never flatters, and is often
scarcely civil to anybody.   He seldom stoops to falsehood;
but if he does, it is to lower other people, and to detract from
that superiority which he thinks unjustly attached to them.

The Vain man is different in nearly all these points.   He is
not sincerely convinced of the superiority he claims.   Seeing
the respect which is paid to rank and fortune, talents or virtues,
he seeks to usurp such respect; and by his dress and mode of
living proclaims a higher rank and fortune than really belong
to him.   He is delighted with viewing himself, not in the
light in which we should view him if we knew all that he
knows, but in that in which he imagines that he has induced
us to view him.   Unlike the proud man, he courts the company of his superiors, enjoying the reflected splendour of
associating with them.   " He haunts the courts of kings and
the levees of ministers, ... he is fond of being admitted to
the tables of the great, and still more fond of magnifying to
other people the familiarity with which he is honoured there;
he associates himself as much as he can with fashionable people,
with those who are supposed to direct the public opinion—
with the witty, with the learned, with the popular; and he
shuns the company of his best friends, whenever the very
uncertain current of public favour happens to run in any respect
against them."   Nevertheless, " vanity is almost always a
sprightly and gay, and very often a good-natured passion."
Even the falsehoods of the vain man are all innocent falsehoods, meant to raise himself, not to lower other people.   He
does not, like the proud man, think his character above improvement; but, in his desire of the esteem and admiration
of others, is actuated by a real motive to noble exertion.
Vanity is frequently only a premature attempt to usurp glory
before it is due; and so "the great secret of education is to

direct vanity to proper objects," by discouraging pretensions to trivial accomplishments, but not those to more important ones.

Both the proud and the vain man are constantly dissatisfied; the one being tormented by what he considers the unjust superiority of other people, and the other dreading the shame of the detection of his groundless pretensions. So that here again the rule holds good; and that degree of self-estimation which contributes most to the happiness and contentment of the person himself, is likewise that which most commends itself to the approbation of the impartial spectator.

It remains, then, to draw some concluding comparisons between the virtues of Self-command and the three primary virtues—Prudence, Justice, and Benevolence.

The virtues of self-command are almost entirely recommended to us by the sense of propriety, by regard to the sentiments of the supposed impartial spectator; whilst the virtues of prudence, justice and benevolence, are chiefly recommended to us by concern for our own happiness or the happiness of other people. They are recommended to us primarily by our selfish or benevolent affections, independently of any regard as to what are or ought to be the sentiments of other people. Such regard indeed comes later to enforce their practice; and no man ever trod steadily in their paths whose conduct was not principally directed by a regard to the sentiments of the supposed impartial spectator, the great inmate of the breast and arbiter of our conduct. But regard for the sentiments of other people constitutes the very foundation of the virtues of self-restraint, and is the sole principle that can moderate our passions to that degree where the spectator will give his approval.

Another difference is, that while regard to the beneficial effects of prudence, justice, and benevolence recommend them

originally to the agent and afterwards to the spectator, no such
sense of their utility adds itself to our sense of the propriety
of the virtues of self-command. Their effects may be agreeable or the contrary, without affecting the approbation bestowed on them. Valour displayed in the cause of justice is
loved and admired, but in the cause of injustice it is still regarded with some approbation. In that, as in all the other
virtues of self-command, it is the greatness and steadiness of the
exertion, and the strong sense of propriety necessary to maintain that exertion, which is the source of admiration. The
effects are often only too little regarded.

CHAPTER X.

ADAM SMITH'S THEORY OF HAPPINESS.

ALTHOUGH Adam Smith never distinctly faces the problem of the supreme end of life, nor asks himself whether virtue and morality are merely means to the attainment of happiness, or whether they are ends in themselves irrespective of happiness, he leaves little doubt that happiness really occupies in his system very much the same place that it does in the systems of professed utilitarians. But he distinguishes between happiness as the natural result of virtue and happiness as the end or purpose of virtue; and, by satisfying himself that it *is* the natural result, he saves himself from considering whether, if it were not, virtue would remain in and for itself desirable as an end.

"The happiness of mankind," he says, "as well as of all other rational creatures, seems to have been the original purpose of the Author of Nature," no other end appearing to be worthy of His supreme wisdom and beneficence. The fact therefore that we most effectually promote the happiness of mankind, and so to some extent promote the great plan of Providence by acting according to the dictates of our moral faculties, is an additional reason, though not the primary one, for our doing so; and, conversely, the tendency of an opposite course of conduct to obstruct the scheme thus ordained for the happiness of the world, is an additional reason for abstaining from it. Accordingly, the ultimate sanction of our

compliance with the rules for the promotion of human welfare—the ultimate sanction, that is, of virtue—lies in a system
of future rewards and punishments, by which our co-operation
with the divine plan may be enforced.

To this extent, therefore, Adam Smith seems to agree with
the utilitarianism of Paley in making the happiness of another
world the ultimate motive for virtuous action in this. But
although he thus appeals to religion as enforcing the sense of
duty, he is far from regarding morality as only valuable for
that reason. He protests against the theory that " we ought
not to be grateful from gratitude, we ought not to be chari-
table from humanity, we ought not to be public-spirited from
the love of our country, nor generous and just from the
love of mankind, and that our sole motive in performing
these duties should be a sense that God has commanded
them."

Hence when he speaks of the perfection and happiness of
mankind as " the great end " aimed at by nature, it is clear
that he intends the temporal and general welfare of the world,
and that, though the happiness of another may be a motive to
virtue, it is not so much the end and object of it as happiness
in this. It is in this life, also, that virtue and happiness, vice
and misery, are closely associated; and nature may be regarded
as having purposely bestowed on every virtue and vice that
precise reward or punishment which is best fitted either to
encourage the one or to restrain the other. Thus the reward
attached to industry and prudence—namely, success in every
sort of business—is precisely that which is best calculated to
encourage those virtues, just as in the same way and for the
same reason there is attached to the practice of truth, justice,
and humanity, the confidence and esteem of those we live with.
It requires indeed a very extraordinary concurrence of circumstances to defeat those natural and temporal rewards or

punishments for virtue or vice, which have been fixed in the sentiments and opinions of mankind.

Adam Smith does not then regard virtue entirely as its own end, irrespective of its recompence in the increase of our happiness. Still less, however, does he acknowledge the cardinal doctrine of the utilitarian school, that virtue derives its whole and sole merit from its conduciveness to the general welfare of humanity. He takes up a sort of middle ground between the Epicurean theory, that virtue is good as a means to happiness as the end, and the theory of the Stoics, that virtue is an end in itself independently of happiness. The practice of virtue, he would have said, is a means to happiness, and has been so related to it by nature; but it has, nevertheless, prior claims of its own, quite apart from all reference to its effect upon our welfare.

There is little attempt on the part of our author at any scientific analysis of human happiness like that attempted by Aristotle, and in modern times by Hutcheson or Bentham. But if we take Aristotle's classification of the three principal classes of lives as indicative of the three main ideas of human happiness current in the world, namely, the life of pleasure, the life of ambition, and the life of contemplation and knowledge, there is no doubt under which of these three types Adam Smith would have sought the nearest approximation to earthly felicity.

The life of pleasure, or that ideal of life which seeks happiness in the gratification of sensual enjoyment, he rejects rather by implication than otherwise, by not treating it as worthy of discussion at all. But his rejection of the life of ambition is of more interest, both because he constantly recurs to it, and because it seems to express his own general philosophy of life and to contain the key to his own personal character.

Happiness, he says, consists in tranquillity and enjoyment.

K

Without tranquillity there can no be enjoyment, and with
tranquillity there is scarcely anything but may prove a source
of pleasure.   Hence the Stoics were so far right, in that they
maintained that as between one permanent situation and
another there was but little difference with regard to real
happiness ; and the great source of all human misery is our
constant tendency to overrate the difference between such
situations.   Thus avarice overrates the difference between
poverty and wealth, ambition that between public and private
life, vain-glory that between obscurity and renown.   " In case
of body and peace of mind all the different ranks of life are
nearly on a level, and the beggar who suns himself by the
side of the highway possesses that security which kings are
fighting for."

The story, therefore, of what the favourite of the king of
Epirus said to his master admits of general application to men in
all the situations of human life.   When Pyrrhus had recounted
all his intended conquests, Cineas asked him, "What does
your majesty propose to do then ? "   "I propose," said the
king, " to enjoy myself with my friends, and endeavour to be
good company over a bottle."   And the answer was, " What
hinders your majesty from doing so now ? "

In the highest situation we can fancy, the pleasures from
which we propose to derive our real happiness are generally the
same as those which, in a humbler station, we have at all
times at hand and in our power.   The poor man's son, " whom
heaven in its anger has visited with ambition," will go
through, in the first month of his pursuit of the pleasures of
wealth, more fatigue of body and uneasiness of mind than he
could have suffered through the whole of his life for the want
of them.   "Examine the records of history, recollect what
has happened in the circle of your own experience, consider with
attention what has been the conduct of almost all the greatly

unfortunate, either in private or public life, whom you have either read of or heard of or remember, and you will find that the misfortunes of by far the greater part of them have arisen from their not knowing when they were well, when it was proper for them to sit still and be contented."

Pope taught the same lesson better and more briefly in his well-known lines :—

> Hope springs eternal in the human breast;
> Man never is, but always to be, blest.

And Horace asked Mecænas the same question long ago :—

> Qui fit, Mecænas, ut nemo quam sibi sortem
> Seu ratio dederit, seu fors objecerit illa
> Contentus vivat?

"What can be added," asks Adam Smith, "to the happiness of the man who is in health, who is out of debt, and has a clear conscience?" And this condition, he maintains, is the ordinary condition of the greater part of mankind. Would you live freely, fearlessly, and independently, there is one sure way: "Never enter the place from whence so few have been able to return, never come within the circle of ambition." The love of public admiration admits of no rival nor successor in the breast, and all other pleasures sicken by comparison with it. It is very true, as was said by Rochefoucault, "Love is commonly succeeded by ambition, but ambition is hardly ever succeeded by love."

The following passage is perhaps the best illustration of our philosopher's view of the objects of ambition. "Power and riches," he says, "are enormous and operose machines contrived to produce a few trifling conveniences to the body, consisting of springs the most nice and delicate, which must be kept in order with the most anxious attention, and which, in spite of all our care, are ready every moment to burst into

pieces, and to crush in their ruins their unfortunate possessor.
They are immense fabrics which it requires the labour of a life
to raise, which threaten every moment to overwhelm the person that dwells in them, and which, while they stand, though
they may save him from some smaller inconveniencies, can
protect him from none of the severer inclemencies of the season.
They keep off the summer shower but not the winter storm,
but leave him as much, and sometimes more, exposed than
before to anxiety, to fear, and to sorrow ; to diseases, to danger,
and to death."

The question then arises, Why do we all so generally flee
from poverty and pursue riches ? The answer is (and it is one
of the happiest applications of the author's favourite theory,
though it equally solves the problem of the great absence of
contentment), from regard to the common sentiments of mankind ; from the greater sympathy or admiration naturally felt
for the rich than for the poor. For being as we are more
disposed to sympathize with joy than with sorrow, we more
naturally enter into the agreeable emotions which accompany
the possessor of riches, whilst we fail of much real fellow-feeling
for the distress and misery of poverty. Sympathy with
poverty is a sympathy of pity; sympathy with wealth a
sympathy of admiration, a sympathy altogether more pleasurable than the other. The situation of wealth most sets a man
in the view of general sympathy and attention ; and it is the
consciousness of this sympathetic admiration which riches
bring with them, not the ease or pleasure they afford, that makes
their possession so ardently desired. It is the opposite consciousness which makes all the misery of poverty ; the feeling
of being placed away from the sight or notice of mankind, the
feeling that a man's misery is also disagreeable to others.
Hence it is that for every calamity or injury which affects the
rich, the spectator feels ten times more compassion than when

the same things happen to other people ; thus all the innocent blood that was shed in the civil wars provoked less indignation than the death of Charles I. ; and hence the misfortunes of kings, like those of lovers, are the only real proper subjects of tragedy, for in spite of reason and experience our imagination attaches to these two conditions of life a happiness superior to that of any other.

But this disposition of mankind to sympathize with all the passions of the rich and powerful has also its utility as the source of the distinction of ranks and of the peace and order of society. It is not the case, as was taught by Epicurus, that the tendency of riches and power to procure pleasure makes them desirable, and that the tendency to produce pain is the great evil of poverty. Riches are desirable for the general sympathy which goes along with them, and the absence of such sympathy is the evil of their want. Still less is the reverence of men for their superiors founded on any selfish expectations of benefit from their good-will. It arises rather from a simple admiration of the advantages of their position, and is primarily a disinterested sentiment. From a natural sympathetic admiration of their happiness, we desire to serve them for their own sakes, and require no other recompense than the vanity and honour of obliging them.

It would equally be a mistake to suppose that the common deference paid to the rich is founded on any regard for the general utility of such submission, or for the support it gives to the maintenance of social order, for even when it may be most beneficial to oppose them, such opposition is most reluctantly made. The tendency to reverence them is so natural, that even when a people are brought to desire the punishment of their kings, the sorrow felt for the mortification of a monarch is ever ready to revive former sentiments of loyalty. The death of Charles I. brought about the Restoration, and sympathy for James II. when he was caught by the populace making his escape on board ship, went very nigh to preventing the Revolution.

But although this disposition to sympathize with the rich is conducive to the good order of society, Adam Smith admits that it to a certain extent tends to corrupt moral sentiments. For in equal degrees of merit, the rich and great receive more honour than the poor and humble; and if it be "scarce agreeable to good morals or even to good language, to say that mere wealth and greatness, abstracted from merit and virtue, deserve our respect," it is certain that they almost always obtain it, and that they are therefore pursued as its natural objects.

Hence it comes about, that "the external graces, the frivolous accomplishments, of that impertinent and foolish thing, called a man of fashion, are commonly more admired than the solid and masculine virtues of a warrior, a statesman, a philosopher or a legislator." Not only the dress, and language, and behaviour of the rich and great become favourable, but their vices and follies too, vain men giving themselves airs of a fashionable profligacy of which in their hearts they do not approve and of which perhaps they are not guilty. For "there are hypocrites of wealth and greatness as well as of religion and virtue; and a vain man is apt to pretend to be what he is not in one way, as a cunning man is in the other."

CHAPTER XI.

IN our sympathy for rank and wealth, as explained in the last chapter, Adam Smith sees plainly the "benevolent wisdom of nature." "Nature," he says, "has wisely judged that the distinction of ranks, the peace and order of society, would rest more securely upon the plain and palpable difference of birth and fortune than upon the invisible and often uncertain difference of wisdom and virtue." And in discussing the perverting influence of chance upon our moral sentiments, he finds the same justification for our admiration of Success. For equally with our admiration for mere wealth it is necessary for the stability of society. We are thereby taught to submit more easily to our superiors, and to regard with reverence, or a kind of respectful affection, that fortunate violence we can no longer resist. By this admiration for success, we acquiesce with less reluctance in the government which an irresistible force often imposes on us, and submit no less easily to an Attila or a Tamerlane than to a Cæsar or an Alexander.

To a certain extent this conception of Nature, and recognition of design, entered into the general thought of the time. Even Hume said, "It is wisely ordained by nature that private connexions should commonly prevail over universal views and considerations; otherwise our affections and actions would be dissipated and lost for want of a proper limited object." But Adam Smith more particularly adopted this

view of things, and the assumption of Final Causes as explana-
tory of moral phenomena is one of the most striking features
in his philosophy ; nor does he ever weary of identifying the
actual facts or results of morality with the actual intention of
nature. It seems as if the shadow of Mandeville had rested
over his pen, and that he often wrote rather as the advocate
of a sytem of nature which he believed to have been falsely
impugned than as merely the analyst of our moral sentiments.
Writing too as he describes himself to have done, with an immense landscape of lawns and woods and mountains before his
window, it is perhaps not surprising, that his observation of
the physical world should have pleasantly affected his contemplation of the moral one, and blessed him with that opti-
mistic and genial view of things, which forms so agreeable a
feature in his *Theory*.

The extent to which Adam Smith applies his doctrine of
final causes in ethics is so remarkable, that it is worth while
to notice the most striking examples of it.

Our propensity to sympathize with joy being, as has been
said, much stronger than our propensity to sympathize with
sorrow, we more fully sympathize with our friends in their
joys than in their sorrows. It is a fact, that however conscious we may be of the justice of another's lamentation, and
however much we may reproach ourselves for our want of
sensibility, our sympathy with the afflictions of our friends
generally vanishes when we leave their presence. Such is the
fact, the final cause of which is thus stated : " Nature, it
seems, when she loaded us with our own sorrows, thought that
they were enough, and therefore did not command us to take
any further share in those of others than was necessary to
prompt us to relieve them."

Another purpose of nature may be traced in the fact, that
as expressions of kindness and gratitude attract our sympathy,

those of hatred and resentment repel it. The hoarse discord-
ant voice of anger inspires us naturally with fear and aversion,
and the symptoms of the disagreeable affections never excite,
but often disturb, our sympathy. For, man having been
formed for society, " it was, it seems, the intention of nature
that those rougher and more unamiable emotions which drive
men from one another should be less easily and more rarely
communicated."

Our natural tendency to sympathize with the resentment of
another has also its purpose. For instance, in the case of a
murder, we feel for the murdered man the same resentment
which he would feel, were he conscious himself, and into
which we so far enter as to carry it out as his avengers ; and
thus, with regard to the most dreadful of all crimes, has
nature, antecedent to all reflections on the utility of punishment, stamped indelibly on the human heart an immediate
and instinctive approbation of the sacred and necessary law of
retaliation.

Resentment within moderation is defensible as one of the
original passions of our nature, and is the counterpart of
gratitude. Nature " does not seem to have dealt so unkindly
with us as to have endowed us with any principle which is
wholly and in every respect evil." The very existence of
society depending as it does on the punishment of unprovoked
malice, man has not been left to his own reason, to discover
that the punishment of bad actions is the proper means to preserve society, but he has been endowed with an immediate and
instinctive approbation of that very application of punishment
which is so necessary. In this case, as in so many others, the
economy of nature is the same, in endowing mankind with an
instinctive desire for the means necessary for the attainment
of one of her favourite ends. As the self-preservation of the
individual is an end, for which man has not been left to the

exercise of his own reason to find out the means, but has been
impelled to the means themselves, namely, food and drink, by
the immediate instincts of hunger and thirst, so the preservation of society is an end, to the means to which man is
directly impelled by an instinctive desire for the punishment
of bad actions.

The same explanation is then applied to the fact, that beneficence, or the doing good to others, as less necessary to society
than justice, or the not doing evil to others, is not enforced
by equally strong natural sanctions. Society is conceivable
without the practice of beneficence, but not without that of
justice. Without justice, society, " the peculiar and darling
care of nature," must in a moment crumble to atoms. It is
the main pillar which upholds the whole edifice, whilst beneficence is only the ornament which embellishes it. For this
reason stronger motives were necessary to enforce justice than
to enforce beneficence. Therefore nature " implanted in the
human breast that consciousness of ill-desert, those terrors of
merited punishment which attend its violation, as the great
safeguard of the association of mankind, to protect the weak,
to curb the violent, and to chastise the guilty."

In the influence of fortune over our moral sentiments, in
our disposition to attach less praise where by accident a good
intention has stopped short of real action, to feel less resentment where a criminal design has stopped short of fulfilment,
and to feel a stronger sense of the merit or demerit of actions
when they chance to occasion extraordinary but unintended
pleasure or pain, Adam Smith again traces the working of a
final cause, and sees in this irregularity of our sentiments an
intention on the part of Nature to promote the happiness of
our species. For were resentment as vividly kindled by a
mere design to injure as by an actual injury, were bad wishes
held equivalent to bad conduct, mere thoughts and feelings

would become the objects of punishment, and a state of universal suspicion would allow of no security even for the most innocent. If, on the other hand, the mere wish to serve another were regarded as equivalent to the actual service, an indolent benevolence might take the place of active well-doing, to the detriment of those ends which are the purpose of man's existence. In the same way, man is taught, by that mere animal resentment which arises naturally against every injury, howsoever accidental, to respect the well-being of his fellows, and, by a fallacious sense of guilt, to dread injuring them by accident only less than he dreads to do so by design.

Let us take next the manifestation of fortitude under misfortune. · A man's self approbation under such circumstances is exactly proportioned to the degree of self-command necessary to obtain it; or, in other words, to the degree in which he can assume with regard to himself the feelings of the impartial and indifferent spectator. Thus a man who speaks and acts the moment after his leg has been shot off by a cannon-ball with his usual coolness, feels, as a reflex of the applause of the indifferent spectator, an amount of self-approbation exactly proportioned to the self-command he exhibits. And thus Nature exactly apportions her reward to the virtue of a man's behaviour. But it is nevertheless not fitting that the reward which Nature thus bestows on firmness of conduct should entirely compensate him for the sufferings which her laws inflict on him. For, if it did so, a man could have no motive from self-interest for avoiding accidents which cannot but diminish his utility both to himself and society. Nature therefore, "from her parental care of both, meant that he should anxiously avoid all such accidents."

This is a good illustration of the difficulties of this kind of reasoning in general. It will be easily seen that it raises

more doubts than it solves. If there really is this parental
care on the part of Nature for mankind, why are her measures
incomplete? If the reward she bestows on fortitude did
entirely compensate for the misfortunes it contends with,
would not all the evil of them be destroyed? And might not
Nature, with her parental care, have made laws which could
not be violated, rather than make laws whose observance
needs the protection of misfortune? It does not solve the
problem of moral evil, to show here and there beneficial results;
it only makes the difficulty the greater. Where there is so
much good, why should there be any evil?

To this question Adam Smith attempts no answer, or thinks
the problem solved by the discovery of some good side to
everything evil. His whole system is based on the theory
that the works of Nature " seem all intended to promote happiness and guard against misery." Against those " whining
and melancholy moralists," who reproach us for being happy
in the midst of all the misery of the world, he replies, not only
that if we take the whole world on an average, there will be
for every man in pain or misery twenty in prosperity and joy,
and that we have no more reason to weep with the one than
to rejoice with the twenty, but also that, if we were so constituted as to feel distress for the evil we do not see, it could
serve no other purpose than to increase misery twofold. This
is true enough; but it is another thing to argue from the fact
to the purpose, and to say that it has been wisely ordained by
Nature that we should not feel interested in the fortune of
those whom we can neither serve nor hurt. For it is to men
whose sympathies have been wider than the average that all
the diminution of the world's misery has been due; and it is
fair, if we must argue about Nature at all, to say that had she
endowed men generally with wider sympathies than she has
done, the misery in the world might have been still more

reduced than it has been, and the sum-total of happiness proportionately greater.

Similar thoughts arise with respect to the following passage, wherein Adam Smith contends, in words that seem a foretaste of the *Wealth of Nations*, that Nature leads us intentionally, by an illusion of the imagination, to the pursuit of riches. "It is well that Nature imposes upon us in this manner. It is this deception which rouses and keeps in continual motion the industry of mankind. It is this which first prompted them to cultivate the ground, to build houses, to found cities and commonwealths, and to invent and improve all the sciences and arts, which ennoble and embellish human life; which have entirely changed the whole face of the globe, have turned the rude forests of nature into agreeable and fertile plains, and made the trackless and barren ocean a new fund of subsistence, and the great high road of communication to the different nations of the earth. . . . . It is to no purpose that the proud and unfeeling landlord views his extensive fields, and, without a thought for the wants of his brethren, in imagination consumes himself the whole harvest that grows upon them. . . . . The capacity of his stomach bears no proportion to the immensity of his desires, and will receive no more than that of the meanest peasant.' The rest he is obliged to distribute among those who prepare, in the nicest manner, that little which he himself makes use of, among those who fit up the palace in which this little is to be consumed, among those who provide and keep in order all the different baubles and trinkets which are employed in the economy of greatness; all of whom thus derive from his luxury and caprice that share of the necessaries of life which they would in vain have expected from his humanity or his justice. The produce of the soil maintains at all times nearly

Cf. Hor. Sat. i. 45-6.

that number of inhabitants which it is capable of maintaining The rich only select from the heap what is most precious and agreeable. They consume little more than the poor; and in spite of their natural selfishness and rapacity, though they mean only their own conveniency, though the sole end which they propose from the labours of all the thousands whom they employ be the gratification of their own vain and insatiable desires, they divide with the poor the produce of all their improvements. They are led by an invisible hand to make nearly the same distribution of the necessaries of life which would have been made had the earth been divided into equal portions among all its inhabitants. . . . . When Providence divided the earth among a few lordly masters, it neither forgot nor abandoned those who seemed to have been left out in the partition. These last, too, enjoy their share of all that it produces. In what constitutes the real happiness of human life, they are in no respect inferior to those who would seem so much above them."

Adam Smith applies the same argument to the condition of children. Nature, he maintains, has for the wisest purposes rendered parental tenderness in all or most men much stronger than filial affection. For the continuance of the species depends upon the former, not upon the latter; and whilst the existence and preservation of a child depends altogether on the care of its parents, the existence of the parents is quite independent of the child. In the Decalogue, though we are commanded to honour our fathers and mothers, there is no mention of love for our children, Nature having sufficiently provided for that. "In the eye of Nature, it would seem, a child is a more important object than an old man, and excites a much more lively as well as a more universal sympathy." Thus, again, with regard to the excessive credulity of children, and their disposition to believe whatever they are told, "nature seems to have judged it necessary for their preservation that they should, for some time at least, put implicit confidence in those to whom the care of their childhood, and of the earliest and most necessary parts of their education, is entrusted."

The love of our country, again, is by nature endeared to us, not only by all our selfish, but by all our private benevolent affections; for in its welfare is comprehended our own, and that of all our friends and relations. We do not therefore love our country merely as a part of the great society of mankind, but for its own sake, and independently of other considerations. "That wisdom which contrived the system of human affections, as well as that of every other part of nature, seems to have judged that the interest of the great society of mankind would be best promoted by directing the principal attention of each individual to that particular portion of it which was most within the sphere both of his abilities and of his understanding."

To sum up our author's application of his theory to his general scheme of ethics. Man, having been intended by nature for society, was fitted by her for that situation. Hence she endowed him with an original desire to please, and an original aversion to offend, his brethren. By teaching him to feel pleasure in their favourable, and pain in their unfavourable regards, she laid, in the reward of their approbation, or the punishment of their disapproval, the foundation of human ethics. In the respect which she has taught him to feel for their judgment and sentiments, she has raised in his mind a sense of Duty, and girt her laws for his conduct with the sanction of obligatory morality. And so happily has she adjusted the sentiments of approbation and disapprobation to the advantage both of the individual and of society, that it is precisely those qualities which are useful or advantageous to the individual himself, or to others, which are always accounted virtuous or the contrary.

CHAPTER XII.

ADAM SMITH'S THEORY OF UTILITY.

THE influence which Hume's philosophy exercised over that of Adam Smith has already been noticed with respect to the fundamental facts of sympathy, and the part played by them in the formation of our moral sentiments. But it is chiefly with respect to the position of Utility in moral philosophy that Adam Smith's theory is affected by Hume's celebrated *Inquiry concerning the Principles of Morals.* Not only are all his speculations coloured by considerations of utility, but he devotes a special division of his book to the "Effect of Utility upon the Sentiment of Approbation."

In Adam Smith's theory, the tendency of any affection to produce beneficial or hurtful results is only one part of the phenomenon of moral approbation, constituting our sense of merit or demerit, while the other part consists in our perception of the propriety or impropriety of the affection to the object which excites it. And as the sense of the merit or demerit of any action or conduct is much stronger than our sense of the propriety or impropriety of affections; stimulating us, not merely to a passive feeling of approbation or the contrary, but to a desire to confer actual reward or punishment on the agent, it is evident that the greater part of moral approbation consists in the perception of utility of tendency.

So far, Adam Smith agrees with the utilitarian theory

but he refuses altogether to assent to the doctrine, that the perception of the utility of virtue is its primary recommendation, or that a sense of the evil results of vice is the origin of our hatred against it. It is true that the tendency of virtue to promote, and of vice to disturb the order of society, is to reflect a very great beauty on the one, and a very great deformity on the other. But both the beauty and the deformity are additional to an already existent beauty and deformity, and a beauty and deformity inherent in the objects themselves. Human society may be compared to " an immense machine, whose regular and harmonious movements produce a thousand agreeable effects. As in any other beautiful and noble machine that was the production of human art, whatever tended to render its movements more smooth and easy, would derive a beauty from this effect; and on the contrary, whatever tended to obstruct them, would displease upon that account; so virtue, which is, as it were, the fine polish to the wheels of society, necessarily pleases ; while vice, like the vile rust, which makes them jar and grate upon one another, is as necessarily offensive."

According to Hume, the whole approbation of virtue may be resolved into the perception of beauty which results from the appearance of its utility, no qualities of the mind being ever approved of as virtuous, or disapproved of as vicious, but such as are either useful or agreeable to the person himself, or to others, or else have a contrary tendency. Adam Smith fully admits the fact, that the characters of men may be fitted either to promote or to disturb the happiness both of the individual himself and of the society to which he belongs, and that there is a certain analogy between our approbation of a useful machine and a useful course of conduct. The character of prudence, equity, activity, and resolution, holds out the prospect of prosperity and satisfaction both to the person himself

and to every one connected with him; whilst the rash, insolent, slothful, or effeminate character, portends ruin to the
individual, and misfortune to all who have anything to do
with him. In the former character there is all the beauty
which can belong to the most perfect machine ever invented
for promoting the most agreeable purpose; in the other there
is all the deformity of an awkward and clumsy contrivance.

But this perception of beauty in virtue, or of deformity in
vice, though it enhances and enlivens our feelings with regard
to both, is not the first or principal source of our approbation
of the one, or of our dislike for the other.

" For, in the first place, it seems impossible that the approbation of virtue should be a sentiment of the same kind with
that by which we approve of a convenient and well-contrived
building; or, that we should have no other reason for
praising a man than that for which we commend a chest of
drawers."

" And, secondly, it will be found, upon examination, that
the usefulness of any disposition of mind is seldom the first
ground of our approbation; and that the sentiment of approbation always involves in it a sense of propriety quite distinct
from the perception of utility."

For instance, superior reason and understanding is a quality
most useful to ourselves, as enabling us to discern the remote
consequences of our actions, and to foresee the advantage or
disadvantage likely to result from them; but it is a quality
originally approved of as just and right, and accurate, and
not merely as useful or advantageous. Self-command, also,
is a virtue we quite as much approve of under the aspect of
propriety, as under that of utility. It is the correspondence
of the agent's sentiments with our own, that is the source of
our approbation of them; and it is only because his pleasure
a week or a year hence is just as interesting or indifferent to

us, as spectators, as the pleasure that tempts him at this moment, that we approve of his sacrifice of present to future
enjoyment. We approve of his acting as if the remote object
interested him as much as the future one, because then his
affections correspond exactly with our own, and we recognize
the perfect propriety of his conduct..

With respect again to such qualities which are most useful
to others—as humanity, justice, generosity, and public spirit—
the esteem and approbation paid to them depends in the same
way on the concord between the affections of the agent and
those of the spectator. The propriety of an act of generosity,
as when a man sacrifices some great interest of his own to
that of a friend or a superior, or prefers some other person to
himself, lies not in the consideration of the good effect of such
an action on society at large, but in the agreement of the
individual's point of view with that of the impartial spectator.
Thus, if a man gives up his own claims to an office which had
been a great object of his ambition, because he imagines that
another man's services are better entitled to it, or if he ex-
poses his life to defend that of a friend which he considers of
more importance, it is because he considers the point of view
of disinterested persons, who would prefer that other man or
friend to himself, that his conduct seems clothed with that
appearance of propriety which constitutes the approbation
bestowed on it. It is the accommodation of the feelings of the
individual to those of the impartial bystander, which is the
source of the admiration bestowed on a soldier, who throws
away his life to defend that of his officer, and who deserves
and wins applause, not from any feeling of concern for his
officer, but from the adjustment of his own feelings to those
of every one else who consider his life as nothing when
compared with that of his superior.

So with regard to public spirit, the first source of our

admiration of it is not founded so much on a sense of its utility as upon the great and exalted propriety of the actions to which it prompts. Take, for instance, the case of Brutus, leading his own sons to capital punishment for their conspiracy against the rising liberty of Rome. Naturally he ought to have felt much more for the death of his own sons than for all that Rome could have suffered from the want of the example. But he viewed them, not as a father, but as a Roman citizen; that is to say, he entered so thoroughly into the sentiments of the impartial spectator, or of the ordinary Roman citizen, that even his own sons weighed as nothing in the balance with the smallest interest of Rome. The propriety of the action, or the perfect sympathy of feeling between the agent and the spectator, is the cause of our admiration of it. Its utility certainly bestows upon it a new beauty, and so still further recommends it to our approbation. But such beauty "is chiefly perceived by men of reflection and speculation, and is by no means the quality which first recommends such actions to the natural sentiments of the bulk of mankind."

Adam Smith also differs from Hume no less in his theory of the cause of the beauty which results from a perception of utility than in his theory of the place assignable to utility in the principle of moral approbation. According to Hume, the utility of any object is a source of pleasure from its suggestion of the conveniency it is intended to promote, from its fitness to produce the end intended by it. Adam Smith maintains, rather by way of supplement than of contradiction, that the fitness of a thing to produce its end, or the happy adjustment of means to the attainment of any convenience or pleasure is often more regarded than the end or convenience itself, and he gives several instances to illustrate the operation of this principle.

For instance, a man coming into his room and finding all
the chairs in the middle, will perhaps be angry with his ser-
vant and take the trouble to place them all with their backs
to the wall, for the sake of the greater convenience of having
the floor free and disengaged. But it is more the arrangement than the convenience which he really cares for, since to
attain the convenience he puts himself to more trouble than
he could have suffered from the want of it, seeing that nothing
was easier for him than to have sat down at once on one of
the chairs, which is probably all he does when his labour is
over.

The same principle applies to the pursuit of riches, under
circumstances which imply much more trouble and vexation
than the possession of them can ever obviate. The poor man's
son, cursed with ambition, who admires the convenience of a
palace to live in, of horses to carry him, and of servants to
wait on him, sacrifices a real tranquillity for a certain artificial
and elegant repose he may never reach, to find at last that
"wealth and greatness are mere trinkets of frivolous utility,
no more adapted for procuring ease of body or tranquillity of
mind, than the tweezer-cases of the lover of toys." Indeed,
there is no other real difference between them than that the
conveniences of the one are somewhat more observable than
those of the other. The palaces, gardens, or equipage of the
great are objects of which the conveniency strikes every one;
their utility is obvious; and we readily enjoy by sympathy
the satisfaction they are fitted to afford. But the conveniency
of a toothpick or of a nail-cutter, being less obvious, it is less
easy to enter into the satisfaction of their possessor. They
are less reasonable objects of vanity than wealth and greatness, and less effectually gratify man's love of distinction. To
a man who had to live alone on a desolate island, it might be
a matter of doubt, " whether a palace, or a collection of

such small conveniences as are commonly contained in a
tweezer-case, would contribute most to his happiness and
enjoyment."

The fact that the rich and the great are so much the object
of admiration is due not so much to any superior ease or
pleasure they are supposed to enjoy, as to the numberless
artificial and elegant contrivances they possess for promoting
such ease and pleasure. The spectator does not imagine
"that they are really happier than other people, but he
imagines that they possess more means of happiness. And it
is the ingenious and artful adjustment of those means to the
end for which they were intended, that is the principal source
of his admiration."   •

Again, the sole use and end of all constitutions of government is to promote the happiness of those who live under
them. But from this love of art and contrivance, we often
come to value the means more than the end, and to be eager
to promote the happiness of our fellows, less from any sympathy
with their sufferings or enjoyment than from a wish to perfect
and improve a beautiful system. Men of the greatest public
spirit have often been men of the smallest humanity, like
Peter the Great; and if a public-spirited man encourages the
mending of roads, it is not commonly from a fellow-feeling
with carriers and waggoners so much as from a regard to the
general beauty of order.

This admits however of a practical application, for if you
wish to implant public virtue in a man devoid of it, you will
tell him in vain of the superior advantages of a well-governed
state, of the better homes, the better clothing, or the better
food. But if you describe the great system of government
which procures these advantages, explaining the connexions
and subordinations of their several parts, and their general
subserviency to the happiness of their society; if you show

the possibility of introducing such a system into his own
country, or of removing the obstructions to it, and setting the
wheels of the machine of government to move with more
harmony and smoothness, you will scarce fail to raise in him
the desire to help to remove the obstructions, and to put in
motion so beautiful and orderly a machine. It is less the
results of a political system that can move him than the
contemplation of an ingenious adjustment of means to ends.

CHAPTER XIII.

THE RELATION OF ADAM SMITH'S THEORY TO OTHER SYSTEMS OF MORALITY.

THE longest and perhaps the most interesting division of Adam Smith's treatise is that in which he reviews the relation of his own theory to that of other systems of moral philosophy. For like all writers on the same difficult subject, he finds but a very partial attainment of truth in any system outside his own, and claims for the latter a comprehensive survey of all the phenomena, which his predecessors had only grasped singly and in detail. Every system of morality, every theory of the origin of our moral sentiments, has been derived, he thinks, from some one or other of the principles expounded by himself. And " as they are all of them in this respect founded upon natural principles, they are all of them in some measure in the right. But as many of them are derived from a partial and imperfect view of nature, there are many of them too in some respects in the wrong."

I. Thus with regard, first, to the nature of Virtue, all the different theories, whether in ancient or in modern times, may, Adam Smith thinks, be reduced to three, according as they make it to consist in Propriety, Prudence, or Benevolence: or in other words, according as they place it in the proper government and direction of all our affections equally, whether selfish or social; in the judicious pursuit of our own private interest and happiness by the right direction of the selfish affections alone; or in the disinterested pursuit of the happiness of others under the sole direction of the benevolent affections.

Adam Smith's own theory differed from all these, in that it took account of all these three different aspects of virtue together, and gave no exclusive preference to any one of them. With Plato, Aristotle, and the Stoics, who made virtue to consist in propriety of conduct, or in the suitableness of the motive of action to the object which excites it, or with such modern systems as those of Lord Shaftesbury or Clarke, who defined virtue as maintaining a proper balance of the affections and passions, or as acting according to the relations or to the truth of things, he so far agreed as to regard such propriety as constituting one element in our approbation of virtue; but he maintained that this propriety, though an essential ingredient in every virtuous action, was not always the only one. Propriety commanded approbation, and impropriety disapprobation, but there were other qualities which commanded a higher degree of esteem or blame, and seemed to call for reward or punishment respectively. Such were beneficent or vicious actions, in which something was recognized besides mere propriety or impropriety, and raised feelings stronger than those of mere approval or dislike, and that was their tendency to produce good or bad results. Moreover, none of the systems which placed virtue in a propriety of affection gave any measure by which that propriety might be ascertained, nor could such a measure be found anywhere but in the sympathetic feelings of the impartial and well-informed spectator.

Plato, Aristotle, and the Stoics, only regarded, in their account of virtue, that part of it which consists in propriety of conduct. According to Plato, the soul was composed of three different faculties—reason, passion, and appetite; and that higher form of justice which constitutes perfect virtue was nothing more than that state of mind in which every faculty confined itself to its proper sphere, without encroaching upon that of any other, and performed its office with precisely that degree of strength which belonged to it. In other words, this justice, the last and greatest of the cardinal virtues, and that which comprehended all the others, meant that exact and perfect propriety of conduct, the nature of which has been already discussed. Nearly the same account of virtue was given by Aristotle, who defined it as the habit of moderation in accordance with right reason; by which he meant a right affection of mind towards particular objects, as in being neither too much nor too little affected by objects of fear. And the Stoics so far coincided with Plato and Aristotle as to place perfect virtue, or rectitude of conduct, in a proper choice or rejection of different objects and circumstances according as they were by nature rendered more or less the objects of our desire or aversion. In this propriety of the mind towards external things consisted the life according to nature, or in other words, the virtuous conduct of life.

No less incomplete than systems which placed virtue in propriety alone were those systems which placed it in prudence, or in a prudential regard for mere personal welfare. Such were the systems of the Cyrenaics and Epicureans in ancient times, and of writers like Hobbes and Mandeville in modern times. According to Epicurus, the goodness or badness of anything was ultimately referable to its tendency to produce bodily pleasure or pain. Thus power and riches were desirable as good things, from their tendency to procure pleasure, whilst the evil of the contrary conditions lay in their close connexion with pain. Honour and reputation were of value, because the esteem of others was of so much importance to procure us pleasure and to defend us from pain. And in the same way the several virtues were not desirable simply for themselves, but only by reason of their intimate connexion with our greatest well-being, ease of body and tranquillity of mind. Thus temperance was nothing but prudence with regard to pleasure, the sacrifice of a present enjoyment to obtain a greater one or to avoid a greater pain. Courage was nothing but prudence with regard to danger or labour, not good in itself, but only as repellent of some greater evil. And justice too was nothing but prudence with regard to our neighbours, a means calculated to procure their esteem, and to avoid the fear that would flow from their resentment.

Adam Smith's first reply to this theory is, that whatever may be the tendency of the several virtues or vices, the sentiments which they excite in others are the objects of a much more passionate desire or aversion than all their other consequences; that to be amiable and the proper object of esteem is of more value to us than all the ease and security which love or esteem can procure us : and that to be odious, or the proper object of contempt, or indignation is more dreadful than all we can suffer in our body from hatred, contempt, or indignation ; and that therefore our desire of the one character and our aversion to the other cannot arise from regard to the effects which either of them is likely to produce on the body.

Secondly, there is one aspect of nature from which the Epicurean system derives its plausibility. " By the wise contrivance of the Author of nature, virtue is upon all ordinary occasions, even with regard to this life, real wisdom, and the surest and readiest means of obtaining both safety and advantage." The success or failure of our undertakings must very much depend on the good or bad opinion entertained of us, and on the general disposition of others to assist or oppose us. Hence the tendency of virtue to promote our interest and of vice to obstruct it, undoubtedly stamps an additional beauty and propriety upon the one, and a fresh deformity and impropriety upon the other. And thus temperance, magnanimity, justice and beneficence, come to be approved of, not only under their proper characters, but under the additional character of the most real prudence and the highest wisdom; whilst the contrary vices come to be disapproved of, not only under their proper characters, but under the additional character of the most short-sighted folly and weakness. So that the conduciveness of virtue to happiness is only secondary, and so to speak accidental to its character; it is not its first recommendation to our pursuit of it.

But if the theories which resolved virtue into propriety or prudence were thus one-sided, the remaining theory—that best represented by Hutcheson—was no less so, which made virtue to consist solely in benevolence, or in a disinterested regard to the good of others or the public generally. So far indeed did Hutcheson carry this theory, that he even rejected as a selfish motive to virtuous action the pleasure of self-approbation, "the comfortable applause of our own consciences," holding that it diminished the merit of any benevolent action. The principle of self-love could never be virtuous in any degree, and it was merely innocent, not good, when it led a man to act from a reasonable regard to his own happiness.

Several reasons seem, indeed, at first sight, to justify the identification of virtue with benevolence. It is the most agreeable of all the affections. It is recommended to us by a double sympathy, and we feel it to be the proper object of gratitude and reward. Even its weakness or its excess is not very disagreeable to us, as is the excess of every other passion. And as it throws a peculiar charm over every action which proceeds from it, so the want of it adds a peculiar deformity to actions indicative of disregard to the happiness of others. Our sense too of the merit of any action is just so

far increased or diminished according as we find that benevolence was or was not the motive of the action. If, for
instance, an act supposed to proceed from gratitude is found
to proceed from the hope of some fresh favour, all its merit is
gone; and so if an action attributed to a selfish motive is
found to have been due to a benevolent one, our sense of its
merit is all the more enhanced. And lastly, in all disputes concerning the rectitude of conduct, the public good,
or the tendency of actions to promote the general welfare, has
always been the standard of reference, that being accounted
morally good which tends to promote happiness, and that bad
or wrong which tends to the contrary result.

These reasons led Hutcheson to the conclusion, that an act
was meritorious in proportion to the benevolence evidenced by
it; hence that the virtue of an action was proportioned to the
extent of happiness it tended to promote, so that the least
virtuous affection was that which aimed no further than at
the happiness of an individual, as a son, a brother, or a
friend, whilst the most virtuous was one which embraced as
its object the happiness of all intelligent beings. The perfection of virtue consisted therefore in directing all our actions
to promote the greatest possible good, and in subjecting all
inferior affections to the desire of the general happiness of
mankind.

The first defect which Adam Smith finds in this theory
of his former teacher is, that it fails to explain sufficiently our
approbation of the inferior virtues of prudence, temperance,
constancy, and firmness. Just as other theories erred in regarding solely the propriety or impropriety of conduct, and
in disregarding its good or bad tendency, so this system erred
by disregarding altogether the suitableness of affections to
their exciting cause, and attending only their beneficient or
hurtful effects.

In the second place, a selfish motive is not always a bad one. Self-love may often be a virtuous motive to action. Every man is by nature first and principally recommended to his own care; and because he is fitter to take care of himself than of any other person, it is right that he should do so. Regard to our own private happiness and interest may constitute very laudable motives of action. The habits of economy, industry, discretion, attention, and application of thought, though cultivated from self-interested motives, are nevertheless praiseworthy qualities, and deserve the esteem and approbation of everybody. On the other hand, carelessness and want of economy are universally disapproved of, not as proceeding from a want of benevolence, but from a want of a proper attention to the objects of self-interest.

And as to the standard of right and wrong being frequently the tendency of conduct to the welfare or disorder of society, it does not follow that a regard to society should be the sole virtuous motive of action, but only that in any competition it ought to cast the balance against all other motives.

It was, again, a general defect of each of the three theories which defined virtue as propriety, prudence, or benevolence, that they tended to give a bias to the mind to some principles of action beyond the proportion that is due to them. Thus the ancient systems, which placed virtue in propriety, insisted little on the soft and gentle virtues, rather regarding them as weaknesses to be expunged from the breast, while they laid chief stress on the graver virtues of self-command, fortitude, and courage. And the benevolent system, while encouraging the milder virtues in the highest degree, went so far as to deny the name of virtue to the more respectable qualities of the mind, calling them merely "moral abilities," unworthy of the approbation bestowed on real virtue. Nevertheless the general tendency of each of these systems was to encourage

the best and most laudable habits of the mind, and it were
well for society if mankind regulated their conduct by the
precepts of any one of them.

This general good tendency of these three theories leads our
author to classify by itself, and to treat in a distinct chapter,
a system which, he says, destroys altogether the distinction
between virtue and vice, and of which the tendency consequently is wholly pernicious, and that is the system, which he
designates as the Licentious System, expounded by Mandeville in the *Fable of the Bees.*

Adam Smith considers that this system, " which once made
so much noise in the world . . . could never have imposed
upon so great a number of persons, nor have occasioned so
general alarm among those who are the friends of better principles, had it not in some respects bordered upon the truth."

Mandeville's famous definition of the moral virtues as " the
political offspring which flattery begot upon pride," was
based on the assumption that morality was not natural to
man, but was the invention of wise men, who, by giving the
title of noble to persons capable of self-denial and of preferring the public interest to their own, won mankind generally, through this subtle flattery, to what they chose to
denominate virtue. Hence whatever men did from a sense of
propriety, or from a regard to what was praiseworthy, they
really did from a love of praise, from pride or vanity. This
love of praise was one of the strongest of man's selfish affections,
and the foundation of the love of honour. In conduct apparently the most disinterested, this selfish motive was present.
If a man sacrificed his own interest to that of his fellows, he
knew that his conduct would be agreeable to their self-love,
and that they would not fail to express their satisfaction by
bestowing on himself the most extravagant praises. The
pleasure he would derive from this source counterbalanced the

interest he abandoned to procure it.   Hence all public spirit, or preference of public to private interest was a mere cheat and imposition on mankind.

The fallacy of this system lies, according to Adam Smith, in a sophistical use of the word vanity—in its application to a remote affinity that prevails between two really very different things.   To desire praise for qualities which are not praiseworthy in any degree, or for qualities praiseworthy in themselves but unpossessed by the individual concerned, is vanity proper ; but this frivolous desire for praise at any price is very different from the desire of rendering ourselves the proper objects of honour and esteem, or of acquiring honour and esteem by really deserving them.   The affinity between these very different desires, of which Mandeville made so much use, lay in the fact that vanity as well as the love of true glory aims at acquiring esteem and approbation ; but the difference consists in this, that the desire of the one is unjust and ridiculous, while that of the other is just and reasonable.

There is also an affinity between the love of virtue and the love of true glory, which gives a certain speciousness to Mandeville's theory.   For there is a close connexion between the desire of becoming what is honourable and estimable, which is the love of virtue, and the desire of actual honour and esteem, which is the love of true glory.   They both have— and herein lies their superficial resemblance to vanity—some reference to the sentiments of others.   Even in the love of virtue there is still some reference, if not to what is, yet to what in reason and propriety ought to be, the opinion of others.   The man of the greatest magnanimity, who desires virtue for its own sake, and is most indifferent about the actual opinions of mankind, is still delighted with the thoughts of what those opinions ought to be, and with the consciousness that though he may neither be honoured nor applauded, he is yet the proper object of honour and applause.

Another feature of Mandeville's system was to deny the existence of any self-denial or disinterestedness in human virtue of any kind. Thus wherever temperance fell short of the most ascetic abstinence, he treated it as gross luxury; and all our pretensions to self-denial were based, not on the conquest, but on the concealed indulgence, of our passions.

Here the fallacy lay in representing every passion as wholly vicious, which is so in any degree and in any direction. There are some of our passions which have no other names than those which mark the disagreeable and offensive degree, they being more apt to attract notice in this degree than in any other. It is not therefore to demolish the reality of such a virtue as temperance, to show that the same indulgence of pleasure which when unrestrained is regarded as blameable, is also present when the passion is restrained. The virtue in such cases consists, not in an entire insensibility to the objects of passion, but in the restraint of our natural desire of them.

The same fallacy underlies the famous paradox that "private vices are public benefits," and that it is not the good, but the evil qualities of men, which lead to greatness. By using the word luxury, as it was used in the fashionable asceticism of his time, as in every respect evil, it was easy for Mandeville to show that from this evil all trade and wealth and prosperity flowed, and that without it no society could flourish. "If," Adam Smith replies, "the love of magnificence, a taste for the elegant arts and improvements of human life; for whatever is agreeable in dress, furniture, or equipage; for architecture, statuary, painting, and music, is to be regarded as luxury, sensuality, and ostentation, even in those whose

M

situation allows, without any inconveniency, the indulgence of those passions, it is certain that luxury, sensuality, and ostentation are public benefits." If everything is to be reprobated as luxury which exceeds what is absolutely necessary for the support of human nature, "there is vice even in the use of a clean shirt, or of a convenient habitation." Hence the whole point of the paradox rests on a loose and unscientific use of the word luxury.

II. To turn now to the other great question of ethics, to the nature of moral approbation, and its source in the mind.

As the different theories of the nature of virtue may all be reduced to three, so all the different theories concerning the origin of moral approbation may be reduced to a similar number. Self-love, reason, and sentiment, are the three different sources which have been assigned for the principle of moral approbation. According to some, we approve or disapprove of our own actions and of those of others from self-love only, or from some view of their tendency to our own happiness or disadvantage; according to others, we distinguish what is fit or unfit, both in actions and affections, by reason, or the same faculty by which we distinguish truth from falsehood; and according to yet a third school, the distinction is altogether the effect of immediate sentiment and feeling, arising from the pleasure or disgust with which certain actions or affections inspire us.

According to Adam Smith, there was again some truth in each of these theories, but they each fell short of that completeness of explanation which was the merit of his own peculiar system.

The self-love theory, best expounded by Hobbes and Mandeville, reduced the principle of approbation to a remote perception of the tendency of conduct upon personal well-being; and the merit of virtue or demerit of vice consisted in their respectively serving to support or disturb society, the preservation of which was so necessary to the security of individual existence.

To this our author objects, that this perception of the good effects of virtue enhances indeed our appreciation of it, but that it does not cause it. When the innumerable advantages of a cultivated and social life over a savage and solitary one are described, and the necessity of virtue pointed out for the maintenance of the one, and the tendency of vice to reproduce the other, the reader is charmed with the novelty of the observation ; " he sees plainly a new beauty in virtue and a new deformity in vice, which he had never taken notice of before; and is commonly so delighted with the discovery, that he seldom takes time to reflect that this political view, having never occurred to him in his life before, cannot possibly be the ground of that approbation and disapprobation with which he has always been accustomed to consider tho.e different qualities."

In the application of the self-love theory to our praise or blame of actions or conduct in past time—as of the virtue of Cato or of the villany of Catiline—there was only an imaginary, not an actual, reference to self; and in praising or blaming in such cases we thought of what might have happened to us, had we lived in those times, or of what might still happen to us if in our own times we met with such characters. The idea which the authors of this theory " were groping about, but which they were never able to unfold distinctly, was that indirect sympathy which we feel with the gratitude or resentment of those who received the benefit or suffered the damage resulting from such opposite characters."

Is the principle of sympathy then a selfish principle? Is

sympathy with the sorrow or indignation of another an emotion founded on self-love, because it arises from bringing the
case of another home to oneself, and then conceiving of one's
own feelings in the same situation?

The answer to this question is important, and is best given
in Adam Smith's own words, as he himself admits that the
whole account of human nature which deduces all sentiments and affections from self-love, seems to have arisen
" from some confused misapprehension of the system of sympathy." His answer, which is as follows, will perhaps not be
thought completely satisfactory : " Though sympathy is very
properly said to arise from an imaginary change of situations
with the person principally concerned, yet this imaginary
change is not supposed to happen to me in my own person
and character, but in that of the person with whom I sympathize. When I condole with you for the loss of your only son,
in order to enter into your grief I do not consider what I, a
person of such a character and profession, should suffer if I had
a son, and if that son was unfortunately to die ; but I consider
what I should suffer if I was really you; and I not only
change circumstances with you, but I change persons and
characters. My grief, therefore, is entirely upon your account,
and not in the least upon my own. It is not, therefore, in the
least selfish. How can that be regarded as a selfish passion,
which does not arise even from the imagination of anything
that has befallen, or that relates to myself, in my own proper
person or character, but is entirely occupied about what relates
to you ?" Yet if a reference to self be the fundamental fact of
sympathy, it would seem that this is equivalent to making a
reference to self the foundation of all moral sentiment; as in
Hobbes' explanation of pity, that it is grief for the calamity
of another, arising from the imagination of the like calamity
befalling oneself. And it is remarkable that the same passage

of Polybius which has been thought to be an anticipation of the theory of sympathy, should have also been quoted by Hume, as showing that Polybius referred all our sentiments of virtue to a selfish origin.

Next to the theory which founded moral approbation in self-love, comes that which founded it in reason. This theory originated in the opposition to the doctrine of Hobbes, who made the laws of the civil magistrate the sole ultimate standards of just and unjust, of right and wrong—implying the consequence, that there was no natural distinction between right and wrong, but that they were the arbitrary creations of law. Cudworth taught, that, antecedent to all law or positive institution, there was a faculty of the mind which distinguished moral qualities in actions and affections, and that this faculty was reason; the same faculty that distinguished truth from falsehood, thus also distinguishing right from wrong. It became therefore the popular doctrine, when the controversy with Hobbes was at its height, that the essence of virtue and vice did not consist in the conformity or nonconformity of actions with the law of a superior, but in their conformity or nonconformity with reason; and reason thus came to be considered as the original source of all moral approbation.

In this theory also Adam Smith recognizes some elements of truth. "That virtue consists in conformity to reason is true in some respects; and this faculty may very justly be considered as, in some sense, the source and principle of moral approbation and disapprobation, and of all solid judgments concerning right and wrong." Induction too is one of the operations of reason, and it is by induction and experience that the general rules of morality are formed. They are established inductively, from the observation in a number of particular cases of what is pleasing or displeasing to our moral

faculties. So it is by reason that we discover those general
rules of justice by which we ought to regulate our actions;
and by the same faculty we form those more indeterminate
ideas of what is prudent, decent, generous, or noble, according
to which we endeavour to model our conduct. And as it is by
these general rules, so formed by an induction of reason, that
we most regulate our moral judgments, which would be very
variable if they depended merely upon feeling and sentiment,
virtue may so far be said to consist in conformity to reason,
and so far may reason be considered as the source of moral
approbation.

This admission, however, is a very different thing from the
supposition that our first perceptions of right and wrong can
be derived from reason. These first perceptions, upon which
from a number of particular cases the general rules of morality
are founded, must be the object of an immediate sense and feeling,
not of reason. " It is by finding in a vast variety of instances
that one tenor of conduct constantly pleases in a certain manner,
and that another as constantly displeases the mind, that we
form the general rules of morality. But reason cannot render
any particular object either agreeable or disagreeable to the
mind for its own sake. Reason may show that this object is
the means of obtaining some other which is naturally either
pleasing or displeasing, and in this manner may render it
either agreeable or disagreeable for the sake of something else ;
but nothing can be agreeable or disagreeable for its own sake,
which is not rendered such by immediate sense and feeling.
If virtue, therefore, in every particular instance, necessarily
pleases for its own sake, and if vice as certainly displeases the
mind, it cannot be reason, but immediate sense and feeling
which in this manner reconciles us to the one and alienates us
from the other."

There remained therefore the theories which made sentiment

or feeling the original source of moral approbation ; and the best exposition of this theory was that given by Hutcheson in his doctrine of the Moral Sense.

If the principle of approbation was founded neither on self-love nor on reason, there must be some faculty of a peculiar kind, with which the human mind was endowed to produce the effect in question. Such a faculty was the moral sense —a particular power of perception exerted by the mind at the view of certain actions and affections, by which those that affected the mind agreeably were immediately stamped with the characters of right, laudable, and virtuous, while those that affected it otherwise were immediately stamped with the characters of wrong, blameable, and vicious.

This moral sense was somewhat analagous to our external senses; for as external bodies, by affecting our senses in a certain way, seemed to possess the different qualities of sound, taste, smell, or colour, so the various affections of the mind, by touching the moral sense in a certain way, appeared to possess the different qualities of right or wrong, of virtue or of vice. The moral sense too was a reflex internal sense, as distinct from a direct internal sense ; that is to say, as the perception of beauty was a reflex sense presupposing the direct sense which perceived objects and colours, so the perception of the beauty or deformity of passions and affections was a reflex sense presupposing the perception by a direct internal sense of the several passions and affections themselves. Other reflex senses of the same kind were, a public sense, by which we sympathize with the happiness or misery of our fellows; a sense of shame and honour; and a sense of ridicule.

One consequence of this analogy between the moral sense and the external senses, and a consequence drawn by Hutcheson himself, was that our moral faculties themselves could not be called virtuous or vicious, morally good or morally evil; for the qualities of any object of sense cannot be applied to the sense itself. An object may have the quality of black or white, but the sense of seeing is not black nor white; and in the same way, though an action or sentiment may appear good or bad, the qualities of goodness or badness cannot attach to the moral faculty which perceives such qualities in nature.

Adam Smith objects to this, that we do recognize something morally good in correct moral sentiments, and that we do consider a man worthy of moral approbation whose praise and blame are always accurately suited to the value or worthlessness of conduct. If we saw a man "shouting with admiration and applause at a barbarous and unmerited execution, which some insolent tyrant had ordered," we should be surely justified in calling such behaviour vicious, and morally evil in the highest degree, though it expressed nothing but a depraved state of the moral faculties. There is no perversion of sentiment or affection we should be more averse to enter into, or reject with greater disapprobation, than one of this kind; and so far from regarding such a state of mind as merely strange, and not at all vicious or evil, we should rather regard it "as the very last and most dreadful stage of moral depravity."

Nor are the difficulties less if we found the principle of moral approbation, not upon any sense analogous to the external senses, but upon some peculiar sentiment, intended for such a purpose; if we say, for instance, that as resentment may be called a sense of injuries, or gratitude a sense of benefits, so approbation and disapprobation, as feelings or emotions which arise in the mind on the view of different actions and characters, may be called a sense of right and wrong, or a moral sense.

For if approbation and disapprobation were, like gratitude or resentment, an emotion of a particular kind, distinct from every other, whatever variations either of them might undergo we should expect them to retain clearly marked and distinguishable general features; just as in all the variations of the emotion of anger, it is easy to distinguish the same general features. With regard to approbation it is otherwise, for there are no common features running through all manifestations of moral approval, or the contrary. "The approbation with which we view a tender, delicate, and humane sentiment, is quite different from that with which we are struck by one that appears great, daring, and magnanimous. Our approbation of both may, upon different occasions, be perfect and entire; but we are softened by the one and we are elevated by the other, and there is no sort of resemblance between the emotions which they excite in us." And, in the same way, our horror for cruelty has no resemblance to our contempt for meanness of spirit.

By his own theory Adam Smith thinks that this difference in the character of approbation is more easily explained. It is because the emotions of the person whom we approve of are different when they are humane and delicate from what they are when they are great and daring, and because our approbation arises from sympathy with these different emotions, that our feeling of approbation with regard to the one sentiment is so different from what it is with regard to the other.

Moreover, not only are the different passions and affections of the human mind approved or disapproved as morally good or evil, but the approbation or disapprobation itself is marked with the same moral attributes. The moral sense theory cannot account for this fact; and the only explanation possible is, that, in this instance at least, the coincidence or opposition of sentiments between the person judging and the person judged constitutes moral approbation or the contrary. When the approbation with which our neighbour regards the conduct of another person coincides with our own, we approve of his approbation as in some measure morally good; and so, on the contrary, when his sentiments differ from our own, we disapprove of them as morally wrong.

If a peculiar sentiment, distinct from every other, were really the source of the principle of approbation, it is strange that such a sentiment " should hitherto have been so little taken notice of as not to have got a name in any language. The word ' moral sense' is of very late formation, and cannot yet be considered as making part of the English tongue. . . . . The word ' conscience' does not immediately denote any moral faculty by which we approve or disapprove. Conscience supposes, indeed, the existence of some such faculty, and properly signifies our consciousness of having acted agreeably to its directions. When love, hatred, joy, sorrow, gratitude, resentment, with so many other passions which are all supposed to be the subjects of this principle, have made themselves considerable enough to get them titles to know them by, is it not surprising that the sovereign of them all should hitherto have been so little heeded that—a few philosophers excepted—nobody has yet thought it worth while to bestow a name upon it?"

In opposition then to the theory which derives moral approbation from a peculiar sentiment, Adam Smith reduces it himself to four sources, in some respects different from one another. "First, we sympathize with the motives of the agent; secondly, we enter into the gratitude of those who receive the benefit of his actions; thirdly, we observe that his conduct has been agreeable to the general rules by which those two sympathies generally act; and last of all, when we consider such actions as making a part of a system of behaviour which tends to promote the happiness either of the individual or of the society, they appear to derive a beauty from this utility not unlike that which we ascribe to any well-contrived machine."

CHAPTER XIV.

THE result of the preceding chapter, in which the relation of
Adam Smith's theory to other ethical theories has been
defined, is that it is a theory in which all that is true in the
" selfish" system of Hobbes or Mandeville, in the " benevolent" system of Hutcheson, or in the " utilitarian" system of
Hume, is adopted and made use of, to form a system quite
distinct from any one of them. It seeks to bridge over their
differences, by avoiding the one-sidedness of their several
principles, and taking a wider view of the facts of human
nature. It is therefore, properly speaking, an Eclectic theory,
if by eclecticism be understood, not a mere commixture of
different systems, but a discriminate selection of the elements
of truth to be found in them severally.

The ethical writers who most influenced Adam Smith were
undoubtedly Hume and Hutcheson, in the way of agreement
and difference that has been already indicated. Dugald
Stewart has also drawn attention to his obligations to Butler.[1]
It would be interesting to know whether he ever read Hartley's *Observations on Man,* a work which, published in 1749—
that is, some ten years before his own—would have
materially assisted his argument. For Adam Smith's account
of the growth of conscience—of a sense of duty, is in reality

[1] *Active and Moral Powers,* vol. i., p. 412.

sely connected with the theory which explains its origin by
: working of the laws of association. From our expe-
ace of the constant association between the acts of others
l pleasurable or painful feelings of our own, according as
sympathize or not with them, comes the desire of ourselves
ising in others similar pleasurable, and avoiding similar
nful, emotions—or in other words, that desire of praise and
aversion to blame which, refined and purified by reference to
an imaginary and ideal spectator of our conduct, grows to be
a conscientious and disinterested love of virtue and detestation
of vice. The rules of moral conduct, formed as they are by
generalization from particular judgments of the sympathetic
instinct, or from a number of particular associations of pleasurable and painful feelings with particular acts, are themselves directly associated with that love of praise or praiseworthiness which originates in our longing for the same
sympathy from other men with regard to ourselves that we
know to be pleasurable in the converse relation. The word
"association" is never once used by Adam Smith, but it is
implied at every step of his theory, and forms really as fundamental a feature in his reasoning as it does in that of the
philosopher who was the first to investigate its laws in their
application to the facts of morality. This is, perhaps, internal evidence enough that Adam Smith never saw Hartley's
work.[1]

But the writer who, perhaps, as much as any other contri-
buted to the formation of Adam Smith's ideas, seems to have

[1] Yet in his *Essay on the External Senses*, of which the date is uncertain, and in his *History of Astronomy*, which he certainly wrote
before 1758, mention is made by Adam Smith of the association of ideas.
It is probable, however, that he was acquainted with the doctrine, not
from Hartley, but from Hume's statement of it in the *Inquiry concerning Human Understanding.*

been Pope, who in his *Essay on Man* anticipated many of
the leading thoughts in the *Theory of Moral Sentiments*. The
points of resemblance between the poet and the philosopher
are frequent and obvious. There is in both the same constant
appeal to nature, and to the wisdom displayed in her laws ;
the same reference to self-love as the basis of the social virtues
and benevolence ; the same identification of virtue with happiness ; and the same depreciation of greatness and ambition
as conducive to human felicity.

Adam Smith's simple theory of happiness, for instance,
reads like a commentary on the text supplied by Pope in the
lines,—

> " Reason's whole pleasure, all the joys of sense,
>   Lie in three words—Health, Peace, and Competence."

Said in prose, the same teaching is conveyed by the philosopher : " What can be added to the happiness of the man
who is in health, who is out of debt, and has a clear conscience ? "

Or, to take another instance. Adam Smith's account of
the order in which individuals are recommended by nature to
our care is precisely the same as that given by Pope. Says
the former : " Every man is first and principally recommended
to his own care," and, after himself, his friends, his country,
or mankind become by degrees the object of his sympathies
So said Pope before him :—

> " God loves from whole to parts : but human soul
>   Must rise from individual to the whole.
>   Self-love but serves the virtuous mind to wake,
>   As the small pebble stirs the peaceful lake ;
>   The centre moved, a circle straight succeeds
>   Another still, and still another spreads ;
>   Friend, parent, neighbour, first it will embrace ;
>   His country next ; and next all human race."

To turn now from the theory itself to the criticisms upon it: it may perhaps be said, that if the importance of an ethical theory in the history of moral philosophy may be measured by the amount of criticism expended upon it, Adam Smith's *Theory of Moral Sentiments* must take its place immediately after Hume's *Enquiry concerning the Principles of Morals.* The shorter observations on it by Lord Kames and Sir James Mackintosh bear witness to the great interest that attached to it, no less than the longer criticisms of Dr. Brown, Dugald Stewart, or Jouffroy, the French moral philosopher. The various objections raised by these writers, all of whom have approached it with that impartial acuteness so characteristic of philosophers in regard to theories not their own, will best serve to illustrate what have been considered the weak points in the general theory proposed by Adam Smith. But in following the main current of such criticism, it is only fair that we should try in some measure to hold the scales between the critics and their author, and to weigh the value of the arguments that have been actually advanced on the one side and that seem capable of being advanced on the other.

First of all, it is said that the resolution of all moral approbation into sympathy really makes morality dependent on the mental constitution of each individual, and so sets up a variable standard, at the mercy of personal influences and local custom. Adam Smith says expressly indeed, that there is no other measure of moral conduct than the sympathetic approbation of each individual. "Every faculty in one man is the measure by which he judges of the like faculty in another;" and as he judges of other men's power of sight or hearing by reference to his own, so he judges of their love, resentment, or other moral states, by reference to his own consciousness of those several affections.

Is not this to destroy the fixed character of morality, and to deprive it—as Protagoras, the Greek sophist, deprived it long ago in his similar teaching that man was the measure of all things—of its most ennobling qualities, its eternity and immutability ? Is it not to reduce the rules of morality to the level merely of the rules of etiquette? Is it not to make our standard of conduct dependent merely on the ideas and passions of those we happen to live with ? Does it not justify Brown's chief objection to the system of sympathy, that it fixes morality "on a basis not sufficiently firm"?

Adam Smith's answer to this might have been, that the consideration of the basis of morality lay beyond the scope of his inquiry, and that, if he explained the principle of moral approbation by the laws of sympathy he appealed to, the facts commanded acceptance, whatever the consequences might be. He would have reasserted confidently, that no case of approbation occurred without a tacit reference to the sympathy of the approver; and that the feeling of approbation or the contrary always varied exactly with the degree of sympathy or antipathy felt for the agent. Therefore, if as a matter of fact every case of such approbation implied a reference to the feelings of the individual person approving, then those feelings were the source of moral judgment, however variable or relative morality might thus be made to appear.

He would also have denied that the consequence of his theory did really in any way weaken the basis of morality, or deprive it of its obligatory power over our conduct. The assertion of such a consequence has been perhaps the most persistent objection raised against his system. Sir James Mackintosh, for instance, makes the criticism, that "the sympathies have nothing more of an *imperative* character than any other emotions. They attract or repel, like other feelings, according to their intensity. If, then, the sympathies continue in mature minds to constitute the whole of conscience, it becomes utterly impossible to explain the character of command and supremacy, which is attested by the unanimous voice of mankind to belong to that faculty, and to form its essential distinction."[3] But as, of all Adam Smith's critics, Jouffroy has been the one who has urged this argument with the greatest force, it will be best to follow his reasoning, before considering the force of the objection.

According to him, no more moral authority can attach to the instinct of sympathy than can attach to any other instinct of our nature. The desire of sympathy, being simply an instinct, can have no claim to prevail over the impulses of our other instincts, whenever they happen to come into conflict, than such as is founded on its possible greater strength. For instance, the instinct of self-love often comes into conflict with, and often prevails over, the instinct of sympathy, the motive of self-interest well-understood being thus superior to our sympathetic impulses both in fact and by right. If then there is a superiority in the instinct of sympathy above all our other instincts, it must come from a judgment of reason, decisive of its title; but since such decision of reason implies a reference to some rule other and higher than instinct, our motive in preferring the inspirations of instinctive sympathy to all other impulses must be derived from this higher motive, or, in other words, from reason and not from instinct. Hence, since the sympathetic instinct bears no signs of an authority superior to that of other instincts, there is no real authority in the motive which, according to Adam Smith, impels us to right conduct. Instead of proving that the instinct of sympathy is the true moral motive, Adam Smith describes truly and beautifully the characteristics of this moral motive, and

[3] *Progress of Ethical Philosophy,* p. 210; compare also Dugald Stewart's *Active and Moral Powers,* vol. i., p. 331.

N

then gratuitously attributes them to the instinct of sympathy.
But he fails to apply to rules of conduct founded upon such
an instinct, that which is the special characteristic of the
moral motive, namely, that it alone is obligatory—alone presents us, as an end to be pursued, an end which *ought* to be
pursued, as distinct from other ends suggested by other
motives, which may be pursued or not as we please. " Among
all possible motives, the moral motive alone appears to us as
one that *ought* to govern our conduct."

Jouffroy applies the same reasoning to Adam Smith's explanation of our moral ideas, those, for example, of *Right* and
Duty. For if the motive of sympathy bears with it no authority, it is evident that it cannot explain ideas both of which
imply and involve a motive of obligation. If duty is obedience
to rules of conduct that have been produced by sympathy,
and these rules are only generalizations of particular judgments of instinctive sympathy, it is plain that the authority
of these rules can be no greater than that of the judgments
which originally gave rise to them. If it is equally a duty to
obey the instinct as to obey the rules it gives rise to, it is
superfluous to explain duty as a sense of the authority of
these rules, seeing that it is already involved in the process of
their formation. And if again it can never be a duty to obey
the instinct, because neither its direction nor the desire of
sympathy which impels us to follow it can ever be obligatory,
it can none the more be a duty to obey the rules which are
founded upon the instinct. The authority of the moral rules
or principles of conduct stands or falls with the authority of
the instinct; for if the latter can enforce obligation to a certain degree, it can enforce it in all degrees; and if it cannot
enforce it to this degree, then it cannot in any. It is
therefore Jouffroy's conclusion, that " there is not, in the
system of Smith, any such thing as a moral law; and it is

incompetent to explain our ideas of duty, of right, and of all other such ideas as imply the fact of obligation."[4]

The question then is, How far is such criticism well-founded? How far is it relevant to the subject-matter of Adam Smith's treatise?

Adam Smith might have replied to Jouffroy's objections by asking whether, putting aside the question of the soundness of his theory of the origin of moral approbation, any theory that accounted for the approbation did not *ipso facto* account for the obligation. He might have said that, if he showed why one course of conduct was regarded as good and another as bad, he implicitly showed why one course was felt to be right and the other to be wrong—why it was felt that one course ought to be followed and the other course ought to be avoided. For the feeling of authority and obligation is involved in the fact of approbation. As it has been well put by Brown, " The very conceptions of the rectitude, the obligation, the approvableness (of certain actions) are involved in the feeling of the approbation itself. It is impossible for us to have the feeling, and not to have these. . . . . To know that we should feel ourselves unworthy of self-esteem, and objects rather of self-abhorrence, if we did not act in a certain manner, is to feel the moral obligation to act in a certain manner, as it is to feel the moral rectitude of the action itself. We are so constituted that it is impossible for us, in certain circumstances, not to have this feeling ; and having the feeling, we must have the notions of virtue, obligation, merit.[5] "

Moreover, Adam Smith expressly pointed out that the difference between *moral* approbation and approbation of all other kinds lay in the impossibility of our being as indifferent about *conduct* as about other things, because conduct, either

[4] *Introduction to Ethics ;* translation, vol. ii., p. 147.
[5] *Lectures on Ethics,* p. 13.

N 2

directly or by our imagination, affected ourselves ; so that the additional strength thus conferred on the feeling of *moral* approbation was quite sufficient to account for that feeling of the imperative and obligatory force which inculcates obedience to moral rules. If there is no authority in an instinct *per se*, it may nevertheless be so constituted and may so operate that the strictest sense of duty may ultimately grow from it and upon it. The obligation is none the less real because it can be accounted for ; nor are the claims of duty any the less substantial because they are capable of being traced to so humble a beginning as an instinctive desire for the sympathy of our fellows.

It may therefore be said, on behalf of Adam Smith, that it is not to weaken the basis of morality, nor the authority of conscience, to trace either of them to their sources in sentiments of sympathy, originally influenced by pleasure and pain. The obligatory nature of moral rules remains a fact, which no theory of their origin can alter or modify ; just as benevolent affections remain facts of our moral being, irrespective of their possible superstructure on instincts of self-interest. If conscience is explicable as a kind of generalization or summary of moral sympathies, formed by the observation of the distribution of praise or blame in a number of particular instances and by personal experience of many years, its influence need be none the less great nor its control any the less authoritative than if it were proved to demonstration to be a primary principle of our moral consciousness.

It is also necessary to remember that Adam Smith carefully restricted the feeling of obligation to the one single virtue of justice, and throughout his treatise avoided generally the use of words which, like "right" and "wrong," seem to suggest the idea of obligation. By the use of the words "proper" and " improper," or "meritorious," as applied to sentiments and conduct, he seems to have wished to convey the idea that he did regard morality as relative to time, place, and circumstance, as to a certain extent due to custom and convention, and not as absolute, eternal, or immutable. Properly speaking, justice, or the abstinence from injury to others, was, he held, the only virtue which, as men had a right to exact it from us, it was our *duty* to practise towards them. The consciousness that force might be employed to make us act according to the rules of justice, but not according to the rules of any other virtues, such as friendship, charity, or generosity, was the source of the stricter obligation felt by us in reference to the virtue of justice. " We feel ourselves," he said, " to be in a peculiar manner tied, bound, and obliged to the observation of justice," whilst the practice of the other virtues " seems to be left in some measure to our own choice." " In the practice of the other virtues, our conduct should rather be directed by a certain kind of propriety, by a certain taste for a particular tenor of conduct, than by any regard to a precise rule or maxim ;" but it is otherwise with regard to justice, all the rules of which are precise, definite, and certain, and alone admit of no exception.

As to the authority of our moral faculties, of our perception, howsoever derived, of different qualities in conduct, it is, in Adam Smith's system, an ultimate fact, as indisputable as the authority of other faculties over their respective objects; for example, as the authority of the eye about beauty of colour, or as that of the ear about harmony of sounds. " Our moral faculties, our natural sense of merit and propriety," approve or disapprove of actions instantaneously, and this approval or judgment is their peculiar function. They judge of the other faculties and principles of our nature; how far, for example, love or resentment ought either to be indulged or restrained, and when the various senses ought to be gratified. Hence they cannot be said to be on a level with our other natural faculties and appetites, and endowed with no more right to restrain the latter than the latter are to restrain them. There can be no more appeal from them about their objects than there is from the eye, or the ear, or the taste with regard to the objects of their several jurisdictions. According as anything is agreeable or not to them, is it fit, right, and proper, or unfit, wrong, and improper. "The sentiments which they approve of are graceful and becoming; the contrary, ungraceful and unbecoming. The very words, right, wrong, fit, proper, graceful, or becoming, mean only what pleases or displeases those faculties."

Hence the question of the authority of our moral faculties is as futile as the question of the authority of the special senses over their several objects. For "they carry along with them the most evident badges of this authority, which denote that they were set up within us to be the supreme arbiter of all our actions, to superintend all our senses, passions, and appetites, and to judge how far either of them was either to be indulged or restrained." That is to say, it is impossible for our moral faculties to approve of one course of conduct and to disapprove of another, and at the same time to feel that there is no authority in the sentiment which passes judgment either way.

Perhaps the part of Adam Smith's theory which has given least satisfaction is his account of the ethical standard, or measure of moral actions. This, it will be remembered, is none other than the sympathetic emotion of the impartial spectator—which seems again to resolve itself into the voice of public opinion. It will be of interest to follow some of the criticism that has been devoted to this point, most of which turns on the meaning of the word *impartial.*

If impartiality means, argues Jouffroy, as alone it can mean impartiality of judgment, the impartiality of a spectator must be the impartiality of his reason, which rises superior to the suggestions of his instincts or passions; but if so, a moral judgment no longer arises from a mere instinct of sympathy, but from an operation of reason. If instinct is adopted as our rule of moral conduct, there must be some higher rule by which we make choice of some impulses against the influence of others; and the impartiality requisite in sympathy is itself a recognition of the insufficiency of instinctive feelings to supply moral rules.

It may be said, in reply to this, that by impartiality Adam Smith meant neither an impartiality of reason nor of instinct, but simply the indifference or coolness of a mind that feels not the full strength of the original passion, which it shares, and which it shares in a due and just degree precisely because it feels it not directly but by reflection. If the resentment of A. can only fairly be estimated by the power of B. to sympathize with it, the latter is only impartial in so far as his feeling of resentment is reflected and not original. His feeling of approbation or disapprobation of A.'s resentment need be none the less a feeling, none the less instinctive and emotional, because he is exempt from the vividness of the passion as it affects his friend. It is simply that exemption, Adam Smith would say, which enables him to judge; and whether his judgment is for that reason to be considered final and right or not, it is, as a matter of fact, the only way in which a moral judgment is possible at all.

The next objection of Jouffroy, that the sympathy of an impartial spectator affords only variable rules of morality, Adam Smith would have met by the answer, that the rules of morality are to a certain extent variable, and dependent on custom. Jouffroy supposes himself placed as an entire stranger in the presence of a quantity of persons of different ages,

sexes, and professions, and then asks, how should he judge of
the propriety of any emotion on his part by reference to the
very different sympathies which such an emotion would
arouse. Lively sensibilities would partake of his emotions
vividly, cold ones but feebly. The sympathies of the men
would be different from those of the women, those of the
young from those of the old, those of the merchant from those
of the soldier, and so forth. To this it might fairly be replied,
that as a matter of fact there are very few emotions with
which different people do not sympathize in very different
degrees, and of which accordingly they do not entertain very
different feelings of moral approbation or the reverse. Each
man's sympathy is in fact his only measure of the propriety
of other men's sentiments, and for that reason it is that there
is scarcely any single moral action of which any two men
adopt the same moral sentiment. That morality is relative
and not absolute, Adam Smith nowhere denies. Nevertheless,
he would say, there is sufficient uniformity in the laws of
sympathy, directed and controlled as they are by custom, to
make the rule of general sympathy or of the abstract spectator
a sufficiently permanent standard of conduct.

It is moreover a fact, which no one has explained better
than Adam Smith, in his account of the growth in every individual of the virtue of self-command, that though our moral
estimate of our own conduct begins by reference to the sympathy of particular individuals, our parents, schoolfellows, or
others, we yet end by judging ourselves, not by reference to
any one in particular so much as from an abstract idea of
general approbation or the contrary, derived from our experience of particular judgments in the course of our life. This
is all that is meant by "the abstract spectator," reference to
whom is simply the same as reference to the supposed verdict
of public opinion. If we have done anything wrong, told a

lie, for example, the self-condemnation we pass on ourselves is the condemnation of public opinion, with which we identify ourselves by long force of habit; and had we never heard a lie condemned, nor known it punished, we should feel no self-condemnation whatever in telling one. We condemn it, not by reference, as Jouffroy puts it, to the feelings of John or Peter, but by reference to the feelings of the general world, which we know to be made up of people like John and Peter. There is nothing inconsistent therefore in the notion of an abstract spectator, " who has neither the prejudices of the one nor the weaknesses of the other, and who sees correctly and soundly precisely because he is abstract." The identification of this abstract spectator with conscience, is so far from being, as Jouffroy says it is, a departure from, and an abandonment of the rule of sympathy, that it is its logical and most satisfactory development. There is no reason to repeat the process by which the perception of particular approving sympathies passes into identification with the highest rules of morality and the most sacred dictates of religion. By reference to his own experience, every reader may easily test for himself the truth or falsity of Adam Smith's argument upon this subject.

It is said with truth, that to make the judgment of an impartial or abstract spectator the standard of morality is to make no security against fallibility of judgment; and that such a judgment is only efficacious where there is tolerable unanimity, but that it fails in the face of possible differences of opinion. But this objection is equally true of any ethical standard ever yet propounded in the world, whether self-interest, the greatest possible happiness, the will of the sovereign, the fitness of things, or any other principle is suggested as the ultimate test of rectitude of conduct. This part of the theory may claim, therefore, not only to be as good as any

other theory, but to be in strict keeping with the vast amount
of variable moral sentiment which actually exists in the
world.

In further disproof of Adam Smith's theory, Jouffroy
appeals to consciousness. We are not conscious, he says, in
judging of the acts of others, that we measure them by reference to our ability to sympathize with them. So far are we
from doing this, that we consider it our first duty to stifle our
emotions of sympathy or antipathy, in order to arrive at an
impartial judgment. As regards our own emotions, also,
there is no such recourse to the sympathies of others ; and even
when there is, we often prefer our own judgment after all to
that which we know to be the judgment of others. Consciousness therefore attests the falsity of the theory that we seek
in our own sensibility the judgments we pass upon others, or
that we seek in the opinions of others the principle of estimation for our own sentiments and conduct.

The truth of the fact stated in this objection may evidently
be conceded, and yet the validity of the main theory be left
untouched. The latter is a theory mainly of the origin of
moral feelings, and of their growth ; and emotions of sympathy which originally give rise to moral feelings may well
disappear and be absent when long habit has once fixed them
in the mind. It is quite conceivable, for instance, that if
we originally derived our moral notions of our own conduct
from constant observation of the conduct of others, we might
yet come to judge ourselves by a standard apparently un-
connected with any reference to other people, and yet really
made up of a number of forgotten judgments passed by us
upon them. Children are always taught to judge themselves by appeals to the sentiments of their parents or other
relations about their conduct; and though the standard of
morality, thus external at first, may in time come to be in-

ternal, and even to be more potent than when it was external, it none the more follows that recourse to such sympathy never took place because it ceases to take place or to be noticed when the moral sentiments are fully formed. In learning to read and write, an exactly analogous process may be traced. The letters which so painfully affected our consciousness at first, when we had to make constant reference to the alphabet, cease at last to affect it at all; yet the process of spelling really goes on in the mind in every word we read or write, however unconscious we may be of its operation. Habit and experience, says Adam Smith, teach us so easily and so readily to view our own interests and those of others from the standpoint of a third person, that " we are scarce sensible" of such a process at all.

Then again, the question has been raised, Is it true that sympathy with an agent or with the object of his action is a necessary antecedent to all moral approbation or the contrary ?

It is objected, for instance, by Brown, that sympathy is not a perpetual accompaniment of our observation of all the actions that take place in life, and that many cases occur in which we feel approval or disapproval, in which consequently moral estimates are made, and yet without any preceding sympathy or antipathy. " In the number of petty affairs which are hourly before our eyes, what sympathy is felt," he asks, " either with those who are actively or with those who are passively concerned, when the agent himself performs his little offices with emotions as slight as those which the objects of his actions reciprocally feel? Yet in these cases we are as capable of judging, and approve or disapprove—not with the same liveliness of emotion indeed, but with as accurate estimation of merit or demerit—as when we consider the most heroic sacrifices which the virtuous can make, or the most

atrocious crimes of which the sordid and the cruel can be
guilty." There must be the same sympathy in the case of
the humblest action we denominate right as in that of the
most glorious action ; yet such actions often excite no sympathy whatever. Unless therefore the common transactions
of life are to be excluded altogether from morality, from the
field of right and wrong, it is impossible to ascribe such moral
qualities to them, if sympathy is the source of our approval of
them.

To this objection, founded on the non-universality of sympathy, and on its not being coextensive with feelings of moral
approbation, Adam Smith might have replied, that there was
no action, howsoever humble, denominated right, in which
there was not or had not been to start with a reference to
sentiments of sympathy. It is impossible to conceive any
case in the most trivial department of life in which approbation on the ground of goodness may not be explained by
reference to such feelings. Brown himself lays indeed less
stress on this argument than on another which has, it must
be confessed, much greater force.

That is, that the theory of sympathy assumes as already
existing those moral feelings which it professes to explain.
If, he says, no moral sentiments preceded a feeling of sympathy, the latter could no more produce them than a mirror,
without pre-existence and pre-supposition of light, could
reflect the beautiful colours of a landscape.

If we had no principle of moral approbation previous to
sympathy, the most perfect sympathy or accordance of passions
would prove nothing more than a mere agreement of feeling ;
nor should we be aware of anything more than in any case of
coincidence of feeling with regard to mere objects of taste,
such as a picture or an air of music. It is not because we
sympathize with the sentiments of an agent that we account

them moral, but it is because his moral sentiments agree with our own that we sympathize with them. The morality is there before the sympathy. If we regard sentiments which differ from our own, not merely as unlike our own, but as morally improper and wrong, we must first have conceived our own to be morally proper and right, by which we measure those of others. Without this previous belief in the moral propriety of our own sentiments, we could never judge of the propriety or impropriety of others, nor regard them as morally unsuitable to the circumstances out of which they arose. Hence the sympathy from which we are said to derive our notions of propriety or the contrary assumes independently of sympathy the very feelings it is said to occasion.

A similar criticism Brown also applies to that sympathy with the gratitude of persons who have received benefits or injuries which is said to be the source of feelings of merit and demerit. If it is true that our sense of the merit of an agent is due to our sympathy with the gratitude of those he has benefited — if the sympathy only transfuses into our own breasts the gratitude or resentment of persons so affected, it is evident that our reflected gratitude or resentment can only give rise to the same sense of merit or demerit that has been already involved in the primary and direct gratitude or resentment. "If our reflex gratitude and resentment involve notions of merit and demerit, the original gratitude and resentment which we feel by reflexion must in like manner have involved them. . . . But if the actual gratitude or resentment of those who have profited or suffered imply no feelings of merit or demerit, we may be certain, at least, that in whatever source we are to strive to discover those feelings, it is not in the mere reflexion of a fainter gratitude or resentment that we can hope to find them. . . . The feelings with which we sympathize are themselves moral feelings or senti-

ments; or if they are not moral feelings, the reflexion of
them from a thousand breasts cannot alter their nature."

Unless therefore we already possessed moral feelings of our
own, the most exact sympathy of feelings could do no more
than tell us of the similarity of our own feelings to those of
some other person, which they might equally do whether they
were vicious or virtuous; and in the same way, the most
complete dissonance of feeling could supply us with no more
than a consciousness of the dissimilarity of our emotions. As
a coincidence of taste with regard to a work of art pre-supposes in any two minds similarly affected by it an independent susceptibility of emotions, distinguishing what is
beautiful from what is ugly, irrespectively of others being
present to share them; so a coincidence of feeling with regard
to any moral action pre-supposes an independent capacity in
the two minds similarly affected by them of distinguishing
what is right from what is wrong, a capacity which each
would have singly, irrespectively of all reference to the feelings of the other. There is something more that we recognize in our moral sentiments than the mere coincidence of
feeling recognized in an agreement of taste or opinion. We
feel that a person has acted not merely as we should have
done, and that his motives have been similar to those we
should have felt, but that he has acted rightly and
properly.

It is perhaps best to state Brown's criticism in his own
words: "All which is peculiar to the sympathy is, that
instead of one mind only affected with certain feelings, there
are two minds affected with certain feelings, and a recognition of the similarity of these feelings; a similarity which far
from being confined to our moral emotions, may occur as
readily and as frequently in every other feeling of which the
mind is susceptible. What produces the moral notions there-

fore must evidently be something more than a recognition of similarity of feeling which is thus common to feelings of every class. There must be an independent capacity of moral emotion, in consequence of which we judge those sentiments of conduct to be right which coincide with sentiments of conduct previously recognized as right—or the sentiments of others to be improper, because they are not in unison with those which we previously recognized as proper. Sympathy then may be the diffuser of moral sentiments, as of various other feelings; but if no moral sentiments exist previously to our sympathy, our sympathy itself cannot give rise to them."

The same inconsistency Brown detects in Adam Smith's theory of moral sentiments relating to our own conduct, according to which it would be impossible for us to distinguish without reference to the feelings of a real or imaginary spectator any difference of propriety or impropriety, merit or demerit, in our own actions or character. If an impartial spectator can thus discover merit or demerit in us by making our case his own and assuming our feelings, those feelings which he thus makes his own must surely speak to us to the same purpose, and with even greater effect than they speak to him. In no case then can sympathy give any additional knowledge : it can only give a wider diffusion to feelings which already exist.

It is therefore, according to Brown, as erroneous in ethics to ascribe moral feelings to sympathy, or the mental reflection by which feelings are diffused, as it would be, in a theory of the source of light, to ascribe light itself to the reflection which involves its existence. "A mirror presents to us a fainter copy of external things; but it is a copy which it presents. We are in like manner to each other mirrors that reflect from breast to breast, joy, sorrow, indignation, and all the vivid emotions of which the individual mind is susceptible ; but though, as mirrors, we mutually give and receive emotions, these emotions must have been felt before they could be communicated."

The objection contained in this analogy of the mirror is perhaps more fatal to the truth of Adam Smith's theory than any other. If a passion arises in every one analogous to, though weaker than, the original passion of the person primarily affected by it; if, for instance, by this force of fellow-feeling we enter into or approve of another person's resentment or gratitude; it seems clear that the original gratitude or resentment must itself involve, irrespective of all sympathy, those feelings of moral approbation, or the contrary, which it is asserted can only arise by sympathy. It is impossible to state this objection more clearly than in the words already quoted from Brown. But when the latter insists on the irregular nature of sympathy as the basis of morality—on its tendency to vary even in the same individual many times in the day, so that what was virtuous in the morning might seem vicious at noon, it is impossible to recognize the justice of the criticism. Adam Smith might fairly have replied, that the educational forces of life, which are comprised in ordinary circumstances and surroundings, and which condition all sympathy, were sufficiently uniform in character to ensure tolerable uniformity in the result, and to give to our notions of morality all that appearance of certainty and sameness which undoubtedly belongs to them.

Adam Smith seems himself to have anticipated one of the difficulties raised in Brown's criticism, namely, the relation of moral approbation to the approbation of another person's taste or opinions. Why should the feeling of approbation be of a different kind when we sympathize with a person's sentiments or actions than when we sympathize with his intellectual judgments? The *feeling* of sympathy being the same in either case, why should the feeling of resultant *approbation* be different?

No one could state more clearly than does Adam Smith the analogy there is between coincidence of moral sentiment and coincidence of intellectual opinion; nor is anything more definite in his theory than that approval of the moral sentiments of others, like approval of their opinions, means nothing more than their agreement with our own. The following are his words: "To approve of another man's opinions is to adopt those opinions, and to adopt them is to approve of them. If the same arguments which convince you convince me likewise, I necessarily approve of your conviction; and if they do not, I necessarily disapprove of it; neither can I possibly conceive that I should do the one without the other. To approve or disapprove, therefore, of the opinions is acknowledged by everybody to mean no more than to observe their agreement or disagreement with our own. But this is equally the case with regard to our approbation or disapprobation of the sentiments or passions of others."

Whence, then, comes the stronger feeling of approbation in the case of agreement of sentiments than in that of agreement of opinion? Why do we esteem a man whose moral sentiments seem to accord with our own, whilst we do not necessarily esteem him simply for the accordance of his opinions with our own? Why in the one case do we ascribe to him the quality of rightness or rectitude, and in the other only the qualities of good taste or good judgment? To quote Brown once more: "If mere accordance of emotion imply the feeling of moral excellence of any sort, we should certainly feel a moral regard for all whose taste coincides with ours; yet, however gratifying the sympathy in such a case

o

may be, we do not feel, in consequence of this sympathy, any morality in the taste which is most exactly accordant with our own."

Adam Smith's answer is, that matters of intellectual agreement touch us much less nearly than circumstances of behaviour which affect ourselves or the person we judge of; that we look at such things as the size of a mountain or the expression of a picture from the same point of view, and therefore that we agree or disagree without that imaginary change of situation which is the foundation of moral sympathy. The stronger feeling of approbation in the one case than in the other arises from the personal element, which influences our judgment of another person's conduct, and which is absent in our judgment of his opinions about things. It will be best again to let Adam Smith speak for himself.

"Though," he says, "you despise that picture, or that poem, or even that system of philosophy which I admire, there is little danger of our quarrelling upon that account. Neither of us can reasonably be much interested about them. They ought all of them to be matters of great indifference to us both; so that, though our opinions may be opposite, our affections may still be very nearly the same. But it is quite otherwise with regard to those objects by which either you or I are particularly affected. Though your judgments in matters of speculation, though your sentiments in matters of taste, are quite opposite to mine, I can easily overlook this opposition; and, if I have any degree of temper, I may still find some entertainment in your conversation, even upon those very subjects. But if you have either no fellow-feeling for the misfortunes I have met with, or none which bears any proportion to the grief which distracts me; or if you have either no indignation at the injuries I have suffered, or none that bears any proportion to the resentment which transports me, we can no longer converse upon these subjects. We become intolerable to one another. I can neither support your company, nor you mine. You are confounded at my violence and passion, and I am enraged at your cold insensibility and want of feeling."

Accordingly, we only regard the sentiments which we share as moral, or the contrary, when they affect another person or ourselves in a peculiar manner; when they bear no relation to either of us, no moral propriety is recognized in a mere agreement of feeling. It is obvious that this explanation, to which Brown pays no attention whatever, is satisfactory to a certain point. A plain, or a mountain, or a picture, are matters about which it is intelligible that agreement or difference should give rise to very different feelings from those produced by a case of dishonesty, excessive anger, or untruthfulness. Being objects so different in their nature, it is only natural that they should give rise to very different sentiments. Independently of all sympathy, admiration of a picture or a mountain is a very different thing from admiration of a generous action or a display of courage. The language of all men has observed the difference, and the admiration in the one case is with perfect reason called *moral*, to distinguish it from the admiration which arises in the other. But when Adam Smith classes "the conduct of a third person" among things which, like the beauty of a plain or the size of a mountain, need no imaginary change of situation on the part of observers to be approved of by them, he inadvertently deserts his own principle, which, if this were true, would fail to account for the approbation of actions done long ago, in times or places unrelated to the approver.

But, even if Adam Smith's explanation with regard to the difference of approbation felt where conduct is concerned from that felt in matters of taste or opinion be accepted as satis-

factory, it is strange that he should not have seen the difficulty of accounting by his theory for the absence of anything
like moral approbation in a number of cases where sympathy
none the less strongly impels us to share and enter into the
emotions of another person. For instance, if we see a man in
imminent danger of his life—pursued by a bull or seeming to
fall from a tight rope—though we may fully sympathize with
his real or pretended fear, in neither case do we for that
reason morally approve of it. In the same way, we may
sympathize with or enter into any other emotion he manifests
—his love, his hope, or his joy—without any the more
approving them or passing any judgment on them whatever
Sympathy has been well defined as " a species of involuntary
imitation of the displays of feeling enacted in our presence,
which is followed by the rise of the feelings themselves."*
Thus we become affected with whatever the mental state may
be that is manifested by the expressed feelings of another
person ; but unless his emotion already contains the element
of moral approbation, or the contrary, as in a case of gratitude
or resentment, the mere fact of sympathy will no more give
rise to it than will sympathy with another person's fear give
rise to any moral approval of it. It is evident, therefore, that
sympathy does not necessarily involve approbation, and that
it only involves *moral* approbation where the sentiments shared
by sympathy belong to the class of emotions denominated
moral.

What, then, is the real relation between sympathy and
approbation? and to what extent is the fact of sympathy an
explanation of the fact of approbation?

It is difficult to read Adam Smith's account of the identification of sympathy and approbation, without feeling that
throughout his argument there is an unconscious play upon

* Bain, *Mental and Moral Science*, p 277.

words, and that an equivocal use of the word "sympathy" lends all its speciousness to the theory he expounds. The first meaning of the word sympathy is fellow-feeling, or the participation of another person's emotion, in which sense we may be said to sympathize with another person's hope or fear; the second meaning contains the idea of approval or praise, in which sense we may be said to sympathize with another person's gratitude or resentment. Adam Smith begins by using the word sympathy in its first and primary sense, as meaning participation in another person's feelings, and then proceeds to use it in its secondary and less proper sense, in which the idea of approbation is involved. But the sympathy in the one case is totally different from the sympathy in the other. In the one case a mere state of feeling is intended, in the other a judgment of reason. To share another person's feeling belongs only to our sensibility; to approve of it as proper, good, and right, implies the exercise of our intelligence. To employ the word "sympathy" in its latter use (as it is sometimes employed in popular parlance) is simply to employ it as a synonym for "approbation;" so that sympathy, instead of being really the source of approbation, is only another word for that approbation itself. To say that we approve of another person's sentiments when we sympathize with them is, therefore, nothing more than saying that we approve of them when we approve of them — a purely tautological proposition.

It cannot therefore be said that Adam Smith's attempt to trace the feeling of moral approbation to emotions of sympathy is altogether successful, incontestable as is the truth of his application of it to many of the phenomena of life and conduct. Yet although sympathy is not the only factor in moral approbation, it is one that enters very widely into the growth of our moral perceptions. It plays, for instance, an important part in evolving in us that sense of right and wrong which is

generally known as Conscience or the Moral Faculty. It is one ⟨
of the elements, just as self-love is another, in that ever-forming
chain of association which goes to distinguish one set of
actions as good from another set of actions as bad. Our
observation in others of the same outward symptoms which
we know in our own case to attend joy or grief, pleasure or
pain, leads us by the mere force of the remembrance of our own
pleasures and pains, and independently of any control of our
will, to enter into those of other people, and to promote
as much as we can the one and prevent the other.

Sympathy accordingly is the source of all disinterested
motives in action, of our readiness to give up pleasures and
incur pains for the sake of others; and Adam Smith was so
far right, that he established, by reference to this force of our
sympathetic emotions, the reality of a disinterested element as
the foundation of our benevolent affections. In the same way,
self-love is the source of all the prudential side of morality;
and to the general formation of our moral sentiments, all our
other emotions, such as anger, fear, love, contribute together
with sympathy, in lesser perhaps but considerable degree.
None of them taken singly would suffice to account for
moral approbation.

Although any action that hurts another person may so
affect our natural sympathy as to give rise to the feeling of
disapprobation involved in sympathetic resentment, and
although an action that is injurious to ourselves may also be
regarded with similar feelings of dislike, the constant pressure
of authority, exercised as it is by domestic education, by
government, by law, and by punishment, must first be
brought to bear on such actions before the feeling of *moral*
disapprobation can arise with regard to them. The association of the pain of punishment with certain actions, and the
association of the absence of such pain (a negative pleasure)

with certain others, enforces the natural dictates of our sympathetic or selfish emotions, and impresses on them the character of morality, of obligation, and of duty. The association is so close and constant, that in course of time the feeling of the approbation or disapprobation of certain actions becomes perfectly independent of the various means, necessary at first to enforce or to prevent them; just as in many other cases our likes and dislikes become free of the associations which first permanently fixed them.

In this way the feeling of moral approbation is seen to be the product of time and slow growth of circumstance, a phenomenon to which both reason and sentiment contribute in equal shares in accordance with the laws that condition their development. Moral approbation is no more given instantaneously by sympathy than it is given instantaneously by a moral sense. Sympathy is merely one of the conditions under which it is evolved, one of the feelings which assist in its formation. It is indeed the feeling on which, more than on any other, the moral agencies existing in the world build up and confirm the notions of right and wrong; but it does of itself nothing more than translate feelings from one mind to another, and unless there is a pre-existent moral element in the feeling so translated, the actual passage will not give rise to it. Sympathy enables one man's fear, resentment, or gratitude to become another man's fear, resentment, or gratitude; but the feeling of moral approbation which attends emotions so diffused, arises from reference to ideas otherwise derived than from a purely involuntary sympathy—from reference, that is, to a standard set up by custom and opinion. A child told for the first time of a murder might so far enter by sympathy into the resentment of the victim as to feel indignation prompting him to vengeance; but his idea of the murder itself as a wrong and wicked act—his idea of it as a deed morally worse than the slaughter of a sheep by a butcher, would only arise as the result of the various forces of education, availing themselves of the original law of sympathy, by which an act disagreeable to ourselves seems disagreeable in its application to others. And what is true in this case, the extreme form of moral disapprobation, is no less true in all the minor cases, in which approbation or the contrary is felt.

The feeling of moral approbation is therefore much more complex than it is in Adam Smith's theory. Above all things it is one and indivisible, and it is impossible to distinguish our moral judgments of ourselves from our judgments of others. There is an obvious inconsistency in saying that we can only judge of other people's sentiments and actions by reference to our own power to sympathize with them, and yet that we can only judge of our own by reference to the same power in them. The moral standard cannot primarily exist in ourselves, and yet, at the same time, be only derivable from without. If by the hypothesis moral feelings relating to ourselves only exist by prior reference to the feelings of others, how can we at the same time form any moral judgment of the feelings of others by reference to any feelings of our own?

But although the two sides of moral feeling are thus really indistinguishable, the feeling of self-approbation or the contrary may indeed be so much stronger than our feeling of approval or disapproval of others as to justify the application to it of such terms as Conscience, Shame, Remorse. The difference of feeling, however, is only one of degree, and in either case, whether our own conduct or that of others is under review, the moral feeling that arises is due to the force of education and opinion acting upon the various emotions of our nature. For instance, a Mohammedan woman seen without a veil would have the same feeling of remorse or of moral disapprobation with regard to herself that she would have with regard to any other woman whom she might see in the same condition, though of course in a less strong degree. In either case her feeling would be a result of all the complex surroundings of her life, which is meant by education in its broadest sense. Sympathy itself would be insufficient to explain the feeling, though it might help to explain how it was developed. All that sympathy could do would be to extend the dread of punishment associated by the woman herself with a breach of the law, to all women who might offend in a similar way; the original feeling of the immorality of exposure being accountable for in no other way than by its association with punishment, ordained by civil or religious law, or by social custom, and enforced by the discipline of early home life. It is obvious that the same explanation applies to all cases in which moral disapprobation is felt, and conversely to all cases in which the sentiment of moral approbation arises.

CL Press

A Fraser Institute Project

https://clpress.net/

Professor Daniel Klein (George Mason University, Economics and Mercatus Center) and Dr. Erik Matson (Mercatus Center), directors of the Adam Smith Program at George Mason University, are the editors and directors of CL Press. CL stands at once for classical liberal and conservative liberal.

CL Press is a project of the Fraser Institute (Vancouver, Canada).

CL Press includes a series called CL Reprints. CL Reprints was undertaken to make selected older works—no longer under copyright, chiefly—more available.

People:

Dan Klein and Erik Matson are the co-editors and executives of the imprint.

Jane Shaw Stroup is Editorial Advisor, doing especially copy-editing and text preparation.

Zachary Yost is Production Manager for CL Reprints.

An Advisory Board:

Jordan Ballor, *Center for Religion, Culture, and Democracy*

Caroline Breashears, *St. Lawrence Univ.*

Donald Boudreaux, *George Mason Univ.*

Ross Emmett, *Arizona State Univ.*

Knud Haakonssen, *Univ. of St. Andrews*

Björn Hasselgren, *Timbro, Uppsala Univ.*

Karen Horn, *Univ. of Erfurt*

Jimena Hurtado, *Univ. de los Andes*

Nelson Lund, *George Mason Univ.*

Daniel Mahoney, *Assumption Univ.*

Deirdre N. McCloskey, *Univ. of Illinois–Chicago*

Thomas W. Merrill, *American Univ.*

James Otteson, *Univ. of Notre Dame*

Catherine R. Pakaluk, *Catholic Univ. of America*

Sandra Peart, *Univ. of Richmond*

Mario Rizzo, *New York Univ.*

Loren Rotner, *Univ. of Austin*

Marc Sidwell, *New Culture Forum*

Craig Smith, *Univ. of Glasgow*

Emily Skarbek, *Brown Univ.*

David Walsh, *Catholic Univ. of America*

Richard Whatmore, *Univ. of St. Andrews*

Barry Weingast, *Stanford Univ.*

Lawrence H. White, *George Mason Univ.*

Amy Willis, *Liberty Fund*

Bart Wilson, *Chapman Univ.*

Todd Zywicki, *George Mason Univ.*

Why start CL Press?

CL Press publishes good, low-priced work in intellectual history, political theory, political economy, and moral philosophy. More specifically, CL Press explores and advance discourse in the following areas:

- The intellectual history and meaning of liberalism.
- The relationship between liberalism and conservatism.
- The role of religion in disseminating liberal understandings and institutions including: humankind's ethical universalism, the moral equality of souls, the rule of law, religious liberty, the meaning and virtues of economic life.
- The relationship between religion and economic philosophy.
- The political, social, and economic philosophy of the Scottish Enlightenment, especially Adam Smith.

www.ingramcontent.com/pod-product-compliance
Lightning Source LLC
Chambersburg PA
CBHW011221120626
46545CB00010B/3092